Will POWER

Will Power

The Most Baffling Bequests, Ludicrous Last Wishes, and Daft Declarations in Final Testaments

SUSAN GOLDENBERG

DUNDURN PRESS

Publisher and acquiring editor: Meghan Macdonald | Editor: Carrie Gleason
Cover designer: Karen Alexiou
Cover image: quill: gstudioimagen1/Freepik; radial: studiogstock/Freepik

Library and Archives Canada Cataloguing in Publication

Title: Will power : the most baffling bequests, ludicrous last wishes, and daft declarations in final testaments / Susan Goldenberg.
Names: Goldenberg, Susan, author.
Description: Includes bibliographical references and index.
Identifiers: Canadiana (print) 20250280590 | Canadiana (ebook) 20250280639 | ISBN 9781459755826 (softcover) | ISBN 9781459755833 (PDF) | ISBN 9781459755840 (EPUB)
Subjects: LCSH: Inheritance and succession—Popular works. | LCSH: Wills—Popular works.
Classification: LCC HB715 .G65 2026 | DDC 332.024/016—dc23

We acknowledge the support of the Canada Council for the Arts and the Ontario Arts Council for our publishing program. We also acknowledge the financial support of the Government of Ontario, through the Ontario Book Publishing Tax Credit and Ontario Creates, and the Government of Canada.

Printed and bound in Canada.

Dundurn Press
1382 Queen Street East
Toronto, Ontario, Canada M4L 1C9
dundurn.com, @dundurnpress

To my parents

The seven ages of man: spills, drills, thrills, bills, ills, pills and wills.
— RICHARD J. NEEDHAM (1912–96), columnist, *The Globe and Mail*, 1964–86, and winner of the Leacock Medal for Humour, 1967

CONTENTS

INTRODUCTION

The inspiration for this book came from a parrot. I'm not joking. In its August–September 2020 issue, *Canada's History* magazine published a story I'd suggested and written about a Victoria, British Columbia, parrot named Louis whose owner had willed him her mansion for his lifetime and the angst this caused real estate developers wanting the property.

I wondered if there were more stories of unusual wills concocted by Canadians just waiting to be discovered, collected, and told together in a book. I researched and researched and found a fascinating variety throughout our great land, recent and past, by well-known and "ordinary" people. We Canadians have in common the ability to write distinctive wills. Taken as a whole, the wills in this book provide a unique look at Canada's history and changing customs, attitudes, and values over the years. To the best of my knowledge, this book is the first of its kind in Canada. You may have heard of a few of the wills but likely not their full stories.

Wills don't have to be a morbid topic, a reminder of our mortality. Broadly speaking, in Canadian culture many people regard death and anniversaries of death as sad and sombre, unlike in other cultures where death is celebrated, as in the Day of the Dead festivals in countries such as Mexico, Brazil, and Guatemala. The implied message in those cultures is that death needn't be feared and, as a natural part of life, should be openly talked about, celebrated, and yes, even mocked.

Wills don't have to be standard boilerplate legalese either; they can be individualistic, even quirky, and still be legally valid in Canada. This book is a collection of unique world firsts, funny, eccentric, vindictive, family-dividing, precedent-setting, dead hand–controlling, and provocative instances of wills I found.

But before we get into what makes each of the stories of wills in this book unique, it will help to have a basic understanding of wills in Canada.

Wills in Canada — A Primer

In Canada, wills and estates are under provincial and territorial jurisdiction, not federal. Each province and territory has its own laws; however, a will made in one Canadian province is generally valid in another.

There are two types of wills. The first is a formal (or attested) will drawn up by a lawyer and witnessed by two persons, or a "will kit," which must be in paper format, signed, and witnessed. The second is a holographic (or handwritten) will. To be accepted as valid, holographic wills must be entirely handwritten and signed by the testator (the person making the will) in ink, not pencil — although as you'll see, there have been exceptions under special circumstances to this rule. No typed portions are permitted, whether on a preprinted form or otherwise. Witnesses aren't required. All three territories and all provinces except British Columbia and Prince Edward Island accept holographic wills. BC and PEI make exceptions for people in the military.

Both types of wills in Canada require probate. Probate is the legal process of proving a will's validity and granting the executor the authority to administer the estate. The process and time frame vary from province to province. With holographic wills, the authenticity of the handwriting and the testator's mental capacity are often looked into during the probate process.

In Canada wills can be contested or challenged, but the success rate is low. "Contest" and "challenge" are often used interchangeably but there's a difference. "Challenge" is a more general term referring to any action taken to question a will's validity, including pre-litigation. "Contest" is a formal legal action to invalidate a will, including going to court. Usually, protests come from people aggrieved that they didn't get more or people who feel they should have got something but didn't. Challenging or contesting a will starts with filing a petition to begin legal proceedings. The petition contains the reasons, along with sworn written evidence in support. To win, an objector must prove there was lack of testamentary capacity or undue influence or fraud, or "improper execution" — that the will wasn't properly signed and witnessed or that the dead person's wishes would harm the public good. In the instance of parents and their offspring, children who believe they got a raw deal can contest on the grounds that their parent failed to meet their "moral obligation." There are examples of all these types of will fights in this book.

Challenging or contesting a will is costly, involving lawyer and "expert witness" fees and supporting documents. And the loser may be ordered to pay the winner's legal costs. It's also time-consuming and can take an emotional toll. Embarrassing, negative, unsavoury details that had been kept private will become public knowledge, as you'll find out in these pages.

And now, the stories.

1

THE TRACTOR FENDER WILL

In case I die in this mess I leave all to the wife

— CECIL GEO HARRIS

On June 8, 1948, Cecil George Harris, a middle-aged Saskatchewan wheat farmer, had a terrible accident when he slipped in a field and became pinned underneath his tractor. All alone, with lifeblood pouring from his gruesome injuries, he summoned the willpower to scratch the sixteen words you see above on the left rear fender of his tractor. In doing so, Harris made history.

As far as is known, Harris's will is unique in terms of location. It is also a case study of how a lawyer must be able to deal with the unusual. Nothing like it had happened before; there were no precedents in Saskatchewan, or anywhere, and admirable ingenuity was used by the Harris family lawyer to get the will accepted by the probate court.

Born March 10, 1892, near London, England, Cecil George Harris ("George" to most people) emigrated on his own to Canada at eighteen and went into farming north of Toronto for a brief time before heading west to the southwestern Saskatchewan wheat belt. He acquired land near the budding community of Rosetown, which held grain elevators for the region, and was located close to the Canadian Pacific Railway line. In addition to growing wheat, Harris co-owned and jointly operated a farm equipment supply store. In all respects, he was living the dream of many immigrant Prairie farmers of the time.

In 1938 he married local teacher Bessie May Dukes, ten years his junior. As was common for female teachers at the time, Bessie was required to give up her job when she married. The couple had two children, David Dean and Donna May. At the time of their father's accident, David was nine and Donna seven.

George was active in community affairs, for many years serving as secretary of the local co-op, which marketed wheat for its farmer-members, and as secretary of the school board. He belonged to the Rosetown lodge of the Independent Order of Odd Fellows, a community-service, non-political, non-sectarian, male-and-female fraternal organization with chapter "lodges" in many countries. Overall, Harris was a well-liked and respected member of his community.

On Tuesday, June 8, 1948, the day he unexpectedly and tragically made legal history, Harris worked his fields in the morning before returning to the family farmhouse around noon for midday "dinner," the big meal of the day on farms, prepared as usual by Bessie. "I'll likely work until late," George told Bessie over dinner. "I expect to be back around ten." Ten o'clock at night is about the time Canada's Prairie light begins to fade in early June.

As he was leaving, George told Bessie he was going to a quarter section (160 acres) of land he owned a short distance north of their homestead. He planned to do field work using a tilling device known as a one-way disc plough or, more commonly, a "one-way." The principal operating distinction of the one-way, as its name implies, is that it can be pulled forward behind a tractor, but it cannot be reversed — a feature that played a key role in the tragedy. Bidding his wife farewell, George climbed onto his tractor, a 1939 Case Model C painted a distinct orange-red colour called "Flambeau Red."

As the hours passed and daytime turned into night, Bessie began to worry when her husband didn't return at the time he had planned, and eventually she headed out to the field in search of him. Upon finding her missing husband, she was met with a terrible sight. George's left leg was wedged almost entirely under the tractor's left rear wheel. The Case Model C's metal wheels were equipped with big, deep V-shaped, four-inch steel lugs, which were used to penetrate the soil and enhance the tractor's pulling/lugging power. But they could also be dangerous, and many farmers were injured or killed by them in such accidents. The lugs on Harris's tractor had sliced his trapped left leg from ankle to hip. Blood had been gushing from the wound for hours.

In search of help, Bessie ran to the nearest farmhouse, which was owned by George Whatley, Harris's farm equipment store partner. It would have been a considerable distance as the farmhouses were quite far apart. Whatley, concluding he'd need assistance to free Harris, drove immediately to get another neighbour, Dan Fullerton. "Get help," Whatley told Fullerton. Then, with his wife and Bessie, Whatley drove to the site of the accident.

Fullerton, meanwhile, fetched his teenage son, Nelson, Nelson's friend Bob Hannay, and Bob's father from a game at a local baseball diamond. "Get your family's tractor to help pull George out," Fullerton ordered Bob as he headed off with Nelson and Mr. Hannay.

Bob Hannay later recalled: "When I arrived, Harris was still trapped in a sitting position between the tractor and the one-way disc. I think what happened was that he was standing behind the tractor and reaching forward to the hand clutch on the left side of the seat to briefly engage reverse gear in an effort to jockey the tractor back and forth while greasing the nipple on the hook-up to the one-way disc. Something went wrong and he got caught by the wheel."

The difficult task of extricating Harris was compounded by the total darkness, strong wind, whirling dust, and a thunderstorm that erupted. The rescuers eventually managed to jack up the tractor and pull Harris out. It was urgent to get him to emergency care at Rosetown's hospital, but the rescuers couldn't make speed because the downpour had turned the dirt road leading to the fields into swamp. "It was impossible to go through with a car," Bob Hannay said, "so I had to use the tractor to tow the car all the way to Highway 7, the gravelled main road to Rosetown."

The community newspaper, *The Rosetown Eagle*, reported that Harris arrived at the hospital at 1:30 a.m. on Wednesday, June 9. He died the following day at 3:00 p.m.

His funeral service was held two days later. *The Rosetown Eagle* wrote: "The service was largely attended, and the floral tributes were many and beautiful. Mr. Harris was eulogized as 'A man of quiet, kindly nature, always willing to assist in community affairs.' He will be greatly missed by all who knew him."

On June 10, while Harris was clinging to life in the hospital, George Whatley and Louis Large, another farmer, were applying grasshopper prevention in the field near where Harris's tractor remained. Large, who hadn't been at Harris's rescue, went to examine the tractor. "Look!" he exclaimed to Whatley, pointing to words scratched into the paint on the left side of the fender. "It seems to be a will!"

Acting on the advice of some friends in town, Whatley drove Harris's tractor to a shed on Harris's farm to get it away from the natural elements. Nothing further was done until the day after Harris's funeral, when Bessie examined the fender and said the handwriting was her husband's. Whatley and some more of Harris's neighbours removed the fender from the tractor and, along with Bessie, took it to the law office of W.S. (William Stanley) Elliott of Rosetown in search of legal advice.

Born in Wolseley, a small town in southeast Saskatchewan, Elliott, fifty-five years old in 1948, had been in practice for twenty-seven years. He'd handled many cases, but nothing like this. As Elliott was well aware, Harris's holographic (handwritten) will, though simply one sentence, did not need to be witnessed by anyone to be accepted by the courts. However, under the law, the original will had to be shown. Therein lay a problem. Would the courts accept a will drawn in such an unusual location?

It had been done in other places before, but not in Saskatchewan. For example, a British court had accepted for probate a will written by a soldier in a trench in the First World War on the back of a photo of his girlfriend. "In the event of my death, I leave all my effects and money to this young lady," the soldier's will had stated. Then there was the 1925 case in which John Barnes, a riverboat pilot in Manchester, England, wrote on an eggshell: "17-25. Mag. Everything I possess. J.B." ("Mag" was his second wife, Margaret.) Probate court rejected the will not on the grounds that it had been written on an eggshell but because "everything I possess" was insufficient to prove that Barnes wanted all his possessions to go to Margaret. Added to that was a case in the same year in which a wealthy Los Angeles man named George Hazeltine asked a nurse to give him her petticoat so he could write a will in his final days. In his "petticoat will" Hazeltine left her and another nurse $10,000 bequests, with the rest of his estate to go to his grand-niece. His will was rejected by probate court. What the will was written on wasn't the issue; it was a beneficiary used as a witness that got the will rejected.

Elliott knew that Harris's non-witnessed holographic will would be considered valid if it met the following criteria:

- There had to be proof that the testator really wrote the will. Confirmation could come from people who were present or, if there were none, people familiar with the author's writing and other handwritten items by that person.
- The testator had to have possessed the mental capacity to create the will.
- The testator had to express their intent to distribute their estate.

It's possible Elliott thought an exception to showing the original might be made in this instance, so he took the fender into his keeping and the same day engaged local professional photographer Vernon Pope to make a contemporaneous photographic record suitable for use in court.

Next, Harris's will had to go through "probate," a court procedure to verify the essentials: that the testator really has passed away and really wrote the will. Elliott drew up a list of George's assets and their value — $13,697.71 total (about $179,200 today).

Elliott submitted sworn affidavits in confirmation that the fender will was genuinely Harris's. William James Garland, manager at the bank Harris went to in Rosetown, submitted Harris's signature card on file at the bank. As for Harris having signed only "George Harris" on the card, whereas he used his first name, "Cecil," in his will, Garland noted, "In my banking experience I have often found that the customer doesn't use his full name, but only one given name and this was Harris's practice."

Elliott himself swore an affidavit pertaining to the authenticity of the writing: "I have done business for Cecil George Harris, and during the course of his business I have examined certain documents on which his signature is written." In a 2014 article in the *Saskatchewan Law Review*, Calgary lawyer and legal historian Geoff Ellwand wrote: "This could have caused problems because it opened him to the possibility of being called as a witness with all the difficulties that might entail since he was the lawyer. However, it appears it was a risk he was willing to take."

Harris had written what is called a conditional will — "In case I die in this mess. . . ." But he didn't die right away. To forestall the court from saying that therefore the will was null and void, Elliott got an affidavit from the attending physician at the hospital, Dr. Grenville G.K. Graham, saying that "Mr. Harris died as a result of the injuries received in the accident."

How Harris managed to scratch out his will on the fender was a matter of central importance. If the will was indeed written in Harris's hand, what did he use to mark the hard surface of the fender? What could a man trapped under a tractor wheel have available to accomplish the task? And furthermore, if he found something to write with, how could an immobilized man get access to the fender? These issues, and the way Elliott managed them, are among the reasons the tractor will is in legal textbooks.

Harris had been undressed at the hospital and his clothes given to young Nelson Fullerton, who took them home and gave them to his father, Dan, one of the men who had rushed to Harris's aid. In the right-hand pocket of the trousers, Dan came across a pocket knife with a folding blade at one end and a puncher at the other. He gave it to George Whatley, who passed it on to Elliott. It wasn't enough to hypothesize that the knife was probably what had been used; it had to be proven that it actually was. Elliott got the following affidavit substantiation:

- From bank manager William Garland: "Because of the clearness of the letters and the fact that the fender is not rusted, in my opinion the writing on the said fender was made very recently, and I would go as far to say was written within the last few days."

- From neighbour and business partner George Whatley: "In my opinion the said knife was the instrument used as there is a sharp pointed belt punch on it which could be used for the writing, and from my examination of the belt punch blade there is indication it was used recently as it is clear, bright, and shining, and free from all dirt or rust. The Deceased had access to the said knife and his physical condition was such when I discovered him on the evening of June 8th, 1948 that he was capable of using the said knife to write the said writings."
- From Louis Large, discoverer of the will: "In my opinion the writing on the said Case tractor fender, from its clearness and lack of rust, could only have been done a few days previous to the 10th day of June, A.D. 1948 [the day on which Large spotted the writing]."
- Lawyer Elliott added to his own affidavit: "From further examination of the said fender, due to the fact that the writing is quite clear in the paint surrounding the writing, I conclude that it was done recently as it is not rusted and is in a good state of preservation."

Another issue Elliott realized had to be explained was how a man caught beneath a tractor's wheel was able to reach the fender with his hand. Whatley supplied the answer: "He was caught in such a manner that his right leg was free, and his body and his arms were free, so that he had the full use of his arms and was capable of using his arms and hands. The left rear fender was pressing against his body and was within easy reach of his hands. He was reclining in such a position when I found him that he could write the said writings."

Whether Harris was legally mentally competent when he did his will was another important issue. Whatley swore in his affidavit that Harris "was conscious and coherent when I arrived at the tractor, during the trip to the hospital, and at the hospital." Dr. Graham, the on-duty hospital doctor, said, "Mr. Harris was conscious and coherent."

The case went to the Surrogate Court of the judicial district of Kerrobert in west central Saskatchewan. Judge Robert E. Nay declared Harris's unique will acceptable. Harris's last wish, "I leave all to the wife," was realized. Nay ordered in a handwritten note: "That Portion of [the] fender on which said will is inscribed to be cut from fender under direction of the Clerk of the Court & such portion to remain on file in Court. Fender after such removal to be returned to Petitioner or her solicitor."

The fender plus Harris's pocket knife remained as "court records" at the Kerrobert courthouse for almost fifty years. In 1997, when the building was being repurposed, the Harris artifacts were turned over to the University of Saskatchewan's Law School, where the fender and knife are on permanent display in a cabinet in the College of Law library as a teaching aid in the college's wills and estates courses of "how a creative mind can successfully adapt to even the most unusual and/or life-threatening circumstances." The "tractor fender will" case is still taught in law schools and written about in legal textbooks around the world, and it even made *Ripley's Believe It or Not!*

The will is famous because of its unique site, but it is also distinctive because of its role in legitimizing holograph wills, formerly regarded as inferior to a standard formal will. As Geoff Ellwand wrote in his *Saskatchewan Law Review* essay:

> The Harris will is also a powerful argument in support of holograph wills as an invaluable legal instrument especially in times of crisis, isolation, or poverty. Almost all jurisdictions, even those such as England where holograph wills are not in the normal course of events acceptable to the courts, recognize this fact by making provision for members of the military on active service and sailors at sea to write valid holograph wills. The Harris will stands for the proposition that there can be times in which an extraordinary testamentary document may be the only available alternative.

It's also a lasting testament to ingenuity, courage, love of family, and the strength of small farming communities in which neighbours come to one another's aid.

2

DILEMMA

On a scale of one to ten in oddness, the story of the will of Nicholas "Nick" Bolianatz, of Regina, Saskatchewan, is a ten-plus.

It's extraordinarily "odd" because at the very time Bolianatz was writing his will leaving Irving Nathaniel Simon one-third of his estate and naming him the executor, Simon was stealing from Bolianatz's bank account.

When Bolianatz died a dilemma arose: Should a person who'd stolen money from him be allowed to be the executor of his estate, and should he receive the bequest? Three courts wrestled with this issue.

Nick decided to write a will in May 1999, aged seventy-nine, after receiving a bequest of $30,000 from his late sister's estate, which he deposited into his bank account. Before then his main source of income was monthly payments from the Canadian federal government's Old Age Security (OAS) and Canada Pension Plan (CPP), totalling $1,150 a month, or $13,800 a year.

Nick's two younger brothers, Joseph ("Joe") and Paul, who went by the surname "Bolen" rather than "Bolianatz," also received $30,000 from the sister's estate. On receipt of their bequests, the three brothers decided to get their affairs in order, which included making their wills. Nick, who had worked as a car dealership serviceman and had limited savings of his own, may have previously thought, "What's the point of making a will? OAS and CPP will end with my death and I don't have much money in the bank."

On May 25, 1999, Nick, Paul, and Joe went together to the long-established general practice Regina law firm of MacLean Keith LLP, which helped them draft their wills. They signed their typed-up documents the next day, May 26. In his will Nick Bolianatz named Irving Nathaniel Simon, then forty-eight and the son of an elderly female friend of Nick's, as executor of his will, directing that Simon first pay the debts, taxes, and charges associated with the estate — standard in a will drawn up by a lawyer — and then distribute the rest equally among himself and Nick's two brothers.

Unbeknownst to Nick, however, Simon was then in the process of stealing almost two-thirds of the money he had received from his sister's estate. Simon somehow had gotten hold of Nick's bank card and personal identification number and between May 9 and May 28 of 1999 removed $19,118 from the old man's bank account through the bank's automated teller machines. The bank's video surveillance camera had recorded Simon's actions, and he was arrested and charged with theft.

On June 29, 1999, two months after Nick did his will, a psychiatrist declared Nick "incompetent due to dementia, unable to manage his affairs" under Saskatchewan's 1978 *Mentally Disordered Persons Act*. As a result, the province's Office of the Public Guardian and Trustee took over managing his financial affairs.

Simon pleaded guilty on June 1, 2000, and was ordered to make full restitution to Nick, payable in monthly installments. By the time Nick died on April 3, 2002, nearly two years later, Simon had only partially repaid the money he'd stolen.

Simon was named as executor of Nick's estate in his will. An executor is responsible for managing the estate, settling debts, and distributing assets. In Canada there's no legal prohibition against someone with a criminal record being executor. But Nick's brother Paul didn't think someone who had stolen from Nick should have control over his estate and went to lawyer W. Timothy Stodalka of MacLean Keith, the law firm that had drawn up Nick's, Paul's, and Joe's wills.

The very day after Nick's death, Stodalka wrote Simon asking him to formally renounce being Nick's executor, saying, "If you fail to do so an application will be made to the court to have you removed." The lawyer reminded Simon of his conviction, adding that "by the time the thefts were discovered Mr. Bolianatz was suffering from dementia and unable to change his will. He would not have named you as executor had he known of the thefts when making his Will."

Simon complied and renounced being executor of Nick's will.

As manager of Bolianatz's finances due to his mental incompetence, Saskatchewan's Office of the Public Guardian and Trustee could have taken over the executor duties, but the office prefers to do so only when no alternative is available. Its priority is the living in need of its protection. In this instance, Nick's brother Paul was available and willing to be executor.

Every province and territory in Canada has a Court of Queen's/King's Bench that deals with non-criminal matters such as contract disputes, bankruptcy, insolvency, personal injury, family disputes — and disputes over wills. Saskatchewan's Court of Queen's Bench (Queen Elizabeth II was then monarch) issued "Letters of Administration with Will Annexed" to Paul Bolen, appointing him "administrator" of his brother's estate. The document gives a person not appointed in a will to manage an estate the authority to do so on the grounds that the appointed executor is "unable or unwilling to act."

Not long afterward, lawyer Stodalka again wrote Simon, this time informing him, "Mr. Bolen is of the view that you should voluntarily renounce your bequest." Along with the letter, the lawyer enclosed a renunciation form for Simon to sign and mail back. "If you fail to do so the administrator will take the matter to court." When Simon didn't respond, Bolen turned to the Court of Queen's Bench for help.

On October 1, 2004, he applied for its aid under Rule 452(d)(1) of Saskatchewan's Queen's Bench Rules, which gives the court's judges the power to speed up proceedings, including imposing time limits and giving orders and directions. Executors, administrators, and trustees of wills find it a quick way to resolve "uncertainties." Bolen asked the court to determine whether Simon's thefts disentitled him to his legacy and, if not, whether the amount Simon still owed under the restitution order could be held back from his bequest. Bolen sent his application in the form of an "Originating Notice," a document that initiates a legal case or application before a court or tribunal.

In support of his application, Bolen filed an affidavit in which he said, "My brother had absolutely no idea that Irving Simon was stealing his money, and I have absolutely no hesitation in saying that if my brother had any inkling that Simon was guilty of fraud, he would have never named him as the executor and/or a beneficiary of his estate."

Simon was sent copies of the documents but didn't respond, so Bolen proceeded to court action at Saskatchewan's Court of Queen's Bench. Although Simon didn't turn up at the hearing, send a lawyer on his behalf, or file a written defence, none of this harmed him.

The judge in the case, Lynn B. Macdonald, sided with Simon and berated Bolen. In her view Bolen was seeking to have his opinion that his brother wouldn't have made Simon his executor and a beneficiary if he'd known of his thefts accepted as fact without supplying anything to support it. She said he hadn't addressed a number of important points:

> What were the circumstances that existed when Mr. Bolianatz included Mr. Simon in his will? What was the relationship between Mr. Simon, his mother, and Mr. Bolianatz? What was the state of Mr. Bolianatz's mental capacity when he made his will? These are just a few of the questions left unanswered.
>
> Since there is no factual underpinning for the application and there is no evidence of fraud by Mr. Simon upon Mr. Bolianatz when he made out his will, the application is dismissed.

Bolen went upward to the Saskatchewan Court of Appeal. The justices assigned to the case were Stuart Cameron, J. (John) Gary Lane, and Robert Richards, a very learned trio. The hearing was held May 4, 2005. This time Paul Bolen didn't appear (he was in failing health), sending his lawyer W. Timothy Stodalka in his place, and while Irving Simon did attend, he said nothing. Simon won in a two-to-one decision, announced February 8, 2006, nine months after the case was heard, with Lane and Richards supporting him and Cameron dissenting.

Justice Lane wrote the lead opinion:

> One may be able to draw a link between the attributes of honesty and trustworthiness to the position of *executor*, but I see no basis for drawing a link between those attributes and the position of *legatee*. To draw such an inference and defeat the bequest in these circumstances would create an unacceptable uncertainty in the administration of estates. Such a precedent could lead to wills being overturned in many everyday circumstances. For example, a bequest "to my faithful spouse" could be overturned when it turns out the spouse was unfaithful.

Justice Richards wrote in support of Justice Lane:

> In my opinion, it does not follow inevitably that a testator will disinherit a person found to be stealing from him or her. A testator's reaction to a theft by a beneficiary would normally be a function of several factors including: his or her relationship with the beneficiary, the relative significance of the theft, the beneficiary's reasons for the theft and, finally, the beneficiary's conduct after the theft comes to light. I expect that many people would not automatically disinherit a person for stealing from them. A beneficiary who is genuinely repentant after a theft is discovered is less apt to be left out of a will than one who shows no remorse.

Justice Cameron disagreed:

> It would take the most extraordinary circumstances — and I am hard pressed to imagine them — to conclude that the

> testator would have bestowed the legacy upon Mr. Simon had he known of what Mr. Simon was up to. After all, Mr. Simon was then in the process of destroying the corpus of the estate. Indeed, I am of the respectful opinion that Mr. Simon is not entitled to the legacy, which is to say he is in no position to successfully lay claim to it because his fraud and theft are so closely related to the legacy as to make it unconscionable for him to do so.

Following Paul Bolen's death on July 1, 2005, a substitute administrator, Jerry Ellis, was appointed for Nick's estate. On April 7, 2006, Ellis applied to the Supreme Court of Canada for "leave to appeal," meaning permission from the Supreme Court to present the case. The Supreme Court is Canada's final court of appeal and listens to appeals only if they raise issues of "public importance," such as Constitution interpretation, conflicting decisions from lower courts, and new legal issues.

Ellis's application said:

> Whether the lower court erred in its decision and the dissenting judgment of Cameron J.A. [Justice of Appeal] should be determined by this Court to be correct — Whether common law equitable [fairness] principles should be an available remedy for the Applicant and extended to fit the facts of this case — Whether the issue of Powers of Attorney that survive an incapacity, resulting in incompetent persons being unable to change their Wills to remove a legacy given to an Attorney who has abused his power, is an issue of national importance that should be considered by this Court.

Irving Simon notified the Court that he "did not intend to file a response." The Court declined to consider the appeal, leaving the way clear for Simon to receive his bequest.

3

THE "OSCARS" WILL

The will of "America's Sweetheart," Toronto-born legendary silent-screen megastar Mary Pickford, who died in 1979 at age eighty-seven, made it crystal clear that the public image she had projected of a perfect private life was in large measure a fairy tale.

At her peak, Mary was the highest paid woman in the world in any profession. She was a versatile actress, beloved for her curly locks and innocent demeanour. She was an early feminist, insisting on top billing and top salary and taking no guff. She was the only woman to be a partner in a Hollywood movie studio, founding United Artists in 1919 with actors Charlie Chaplin and Douglas Fairbanks along with filmmaker D.W. Griffith. She was a leading figure in the creation of the Academy of Motion Picture Arts and Sciences (AMPAS) and its Academy Awards, colloquially called the Oscars. She could be a generous philanthropist.

Yet this astute woman, who portrayed herself as a loving mother to two children whom she and her third husband, actor-bandleader Charles "Buddy" Rogers, adopted, showed in her will that she wasn't entirely what she seemed. A loosely worded clause in her will set off a battle over possession of her two Oscars that went to court. And Buddy Rogers, whose public image was of a devoted husband, turned out to be a conniving schemer regarding her will.

Mary's birth name was Gladys Louise Smith. The eldest of three children, she was born in 1892 at 211 University Avenue, now part of Toronto's Hospital for Sick Children. Gladys's family was impoverished, and her early life was hard. In her early years she had diphtheria, pneumonia, and tuberculosis. Her father, John Charles, who died when Gladys was six, was an alcoholic who worked a variety of odd jobs, never holding one for long. Her widowed mother, Charlotte, took in boarders to make money. One of them, a Mr. Murphy, was the stage manager of a small theatre stock company, and he hired Gladys and her sister, Lottie, for bit parts. Over the next decade, Gladys, Lottie, and their brother, Jack, chaperoned by their mother, travelled Ontario and then the U.S. by rail in third-rate stock companies and productions. They were often out of work.

American cinema was in its infancy in the first decade of the 1900s and based in New York City. No talkies, only silents. Gladys auditioned at the Biograph Company, where she impressed director D.W. Griffith, an influential figure in the development of the movie industry, and was hired to be part of Biograph's roster of actors. Griffith thought "Gladys Smith" lacked pizzazz and had her change her name to Mary Pickford. She was petite, five feet tall, pretty with long blonde curls, talented, equally good in drama and comedy, and willing to work in anything and everything so as to make her face familiar to the public. Appearing in over 160 films, starring in fifty-one of them, and becoming an audience favourite worldwide, Mary Pickford became "the first globally recognized movie superstar."

She knew her worth and was strong-willed. In what was a male-run industry, she successfully negotiated for a record amount of money — $10,000 a week, top billing, full control over production of movies in which she starred, and half of a movie's gross profit.

Mary's first marriage was in 1911 to actor Owen Moore. They divorced March 2, 1920, and a few weeks later, on March 28, she married actor Douglas Fairbanks, with whom she'd been having an affair and who divorced his first wife to wed Mary. Such behaviour likely would have destroyed the careers of less popular actors, but Mary and Douglas were mobbed by fans.

Fairbanks bought her a home, a former hunting lodge in Beverly Hills, which they converted and enlarged into a four-storey, twenty-five-room, mock Tudor-style mansion that came to be known as "Pickfair." There were six bedrooms, a glassed-in sun porch, a bowling alley, a billiards room, an Old West-style saloon, servants' quarters, and a large guest wing. The grounds covered eighteen acres, and there were garages, stables, tennis courts, and an in-ground swimming pool, a first for private homes in the Los Angeles area, in which the couple paddled in a canoe for a publicity shot.

Life magazine described Pickfair as "a gathering place only slightly less important than the White House … and much more fun." Dinner guests included Hollywood's A-list, President Franklin Roosevelt and his wife, Eleanor, the Duke and Duchess of Windsor, George Bernard Shaw, Albert Einstein, Helen Keller, Amelia Earhart, Arthur Conan Doyle, Thomas Edison, the king and queen of Siam, and Charles Lindbergh.

The romance didn't last forever. Mary and Douglas separated in 1933 and divorced in 1936. Mary retained Pickfair and in 1937 married Buddy Rogers, twelve years her junior, whom she'd met co-starring in the 1927 film *My Best Girl*.

After her retirement as an actress, Mary and Buddy adopted two children, both from a "foundling home" — ten-year-old Ronald "Ronnie" Charles and an infant girl they named Roxanne.

As the years passed, Mary became reclusive and reputedly a heavy drinker, like her father. She died on May 29, 1979, after suffering a cerebral hemorrhage at Pickfair. Court papers gave the value of her estate at $10.3 million ($43.7 million today), but its true value was estimated to be four times greater. Her thirty-page will, dated June 7, 1971, and five codicils (supplementary documents) dated through 1978, left the bulk of her multi-million-dollar estate to a foundation to be established and named after her, the Mary Pickford Foundation — a mixture, it could be said, of do-goodery and of memorializing herself in perpetuity. A poor girl who became immensely wealthy, she asked that the Mary Pickford Foundation seek ways to use her money to "lessen neighborhood tensions or to eliminate prejudice and discrimination or defend human and civil rights or to combat community deterioration and juvenile delinquency." The foundation still exists and supports education, science, and the arts.

Mary willed Buddy $25,000 in cash plus much of her personal property, some of her real estate holdings, and $48,000 a year in income in a trust set up for him. Besides Rogers, the principal single beneficiary was a niece, Gwynne Pickford Ornstein of Los Angeles. The will set up a $200,000 trust for her and a $150,000 trust for her children. It also provided a $5,000 bequest to Douglas Fairbanks Jr., the namesake son of her second husband from his marriage prior to the one with Mary.

To the Smithsonian Institution in Washington, DC, she left her star sapphire and semi-precious stones; costumes from the motion pictures in which she appeared; pistols, daggers, and antique guns that once belonged to Rudolph Valentino; and a set of Japanese swords to be given as a memorial to former husband Douglas Fairbanks Sr., who'd died in 1939 at age fifty-six. She left her personal clothing to the Motion Picture Relief Fund, which she'd established, and to the Assistance League of Southern California.

But what about her two adopted children, Ronnie and Roxanne? In a June 6, 1979, story about the will, *Los Angeles Times* staff writer Claudia Luther wrote: "The will and codicils are interesting for the lack of provision for the two children adopted by Miss Pickford and Rogers. The will provides only that the two children receive $50,000 each."

Why? The answer appears to be that the acquisition of the children wasn't the lovely fairy tale that Pickford had woven for reporters. A PBS *American Experience* documentary on Mary in 2005 said,

> The children's life in a Hollywood mansion wasn't normal.... Pickford and Rogers treated the children like theatrical props, sending them to boarding-schools and posing them in family photographs when they were home on visits. Pickford became critical of their physical imperfections, including Ronnie's small stature and Roxanne's crooked teeth. Both children would later remark that their mother was too self-interested to provide genuine maternal love.

> As Ronnie entered adolescence, he became cold and surly towards his mother. His sister grew rebellious. Both children married in their late teens, and Ronnie became so troubled that he once attempted suicide. Pickford went to see him in the hospital, complaining, he later maintained, that he had interrupted a well-needed rest she was taking. It was at this point that the children faded from the public eye. Pickford and Rogers stopped talking about them and their friends stopped asking.

On March 30, 2013, Alicia Mayer, a descendant of movie mogul Louis B. Mayer of Metro-Goldwyn-Mayer, posted an online article ironically titled "The Perfect Pickford Family" on the website The Film Colony. To what *American Experience* had said, she added further sad details: "According to one of his [Ron's] children, who contacted me out of the blue, Ron became involved in drug running for a bike gang, and did hard time in a federal prison. He died a toothless drifter, never reuniting with his own family."

Mary did leave some money in trust for her grandchildren, however.

Under the terms of her will, the trustees of the Mary Pickford Foundation, Edward G. Stotsenberg, her accountant during the last twenty years of her life; lawyer Sull Lawrence; and Buddy Rogers were given the option to sell Pickfair to benefit the foundation. The will said that Rogers "can have such household furnishings as he designates as necessary to furnish his [new] home." This loosely worded sentence unwittingly caused a lot of trouble, as Rogers had a much broader interpretation than the two other trustees.

Stotsenberg and Lawrence hadn't reckoned that Rogers's new "lodge," as he called it, which he was building on Pickfair's grounds, would grow like topsy to an estimated 7,500 square feet. "We were placed in an awkward position," Lawrence said. "Both Mary and we assumed that Buddy would want to furnish a much more modest home. Mary would never have gone along with us specifying exactly every single stick of furniture he was to have or have not. She wanted him to be comfortable, but she wanted the foundation to benefit as well."

California's deputy attorney general, William Abbey, who was called in as a watchdog because money had been left to a charitable foundation, said, "We objected to Mr. Rogers's original request for all the furniture. I thought he was over-reaching and I guess the trustees [Stotsenberg and Lawrence] weren't too thrilled either. There was a lot of hard bargaining going on."

While the dispute was raging over who got what, appraisers were going through Pickfair's treasures with a fine-tooth comb. One morning, two moving men arrived to carry some articles from the house across the way to Rogers's home. When asked who they were working for, one replied, "Mrs. Rogers sent us."

"But she's been dead for nearly two years," the appraisers pointed out. The woman the movers likely saw was Beverly Ricono, whom both Mary and Buddy had known for many years. Beverly was a real estate agent in Palm Springs, California, where Mary and Buddy had a second home. Beverly was born in 1927 and was thirteen years younger than Rogers, who'd been twelve years younger than Mary. Buddy and Beverly married on July 23, 1981.

Other precious Pickfair items, including pieces from Mary's exquisite jade collection, never were obtained by the foundation, reportedly stolen by domestic workers during clean-up operations and hidden in the shrubbery to be picked up when nobody else was nearby.

Appraisers spent more than four months cataloguing Pickfair's contents. Dena Hall, one of the appraisers, said she found "a dust-covered 'honeymoon box' 21 inches wide and 6 inches high in a cobwebby closet. I really got the creeps as we opened it. In it we found Mary's flapper-style wedding dress when she married Douglas Fairbanks, a Chinese silk kimono monogrammed DF, negligees, a brown teddy bear, a rag doll, and a picture of the 5-year-old Gladys Smith [Pickford's birth name] taken in Toronto." Bundles of letters written by Mary to Fairbanks pleading with him not to divorce her and besmirch their image of America's perfect couple, Hollywood's royalty, were put up for auction, as were oil paintings of Pickford, Fairbank's costumes from his swashbuckling hit movie *The Mark of Zorro*, some of her costumes, silver from Tiffany's, personally autographed pictures from other Hollywood stars, two solid-gold Cartier monogrammed vanity sets, and some guns that had been owned by Rudolph Valentino.

Pickfair the building was bought by real estate tycoon Jerry Buss, owner of the Los Angeles Lakers basketball team and the Los Angeles Kings hockey team. He paid $5.4 million for the mansion and 2.7 acres of what had been an eighteen-acre estate. He got the bricks and mortar, the shell of the house, but not the considerable contents. As the February 19, 1981, date neared for the auction of Pickfair's contents for the benefit of the Mary Pickford Foundation at the James Goodman Gallery, a Los Angeles–area fine art appraiser and auctioneer, a settlement was reached between Rogers and his two opponents via the probate court following a full year of bickering.

Rogers received $1 million cash for "helping Mary sell her interest in United Artists 25 years earlier." Lawrence and Stotsenberg agreed to the amount in lieu of Rogers getting a share of "community assets," which could have been considerably higher. ("Community assets" means any real or personal property acquired by either spouse during a marriage.) Since Pickford's estate was worth at minimum $10 million, Rogers's share of the community assets would have been more than $1 million, and the foundation would have wound up with far less than it did. Plus, the feud that had been kept out of the public eye was certain to become public knowledge around the time of the auction, which both sides realized would be bad. "We didn't want to get into an embarrassing imbroglio," Lawrence said.

What Rogers ended up with were some of the more publicized contents: a hundred-piece Napoleon and Josephine dinner service specifically willed to him by Mary, ten "Frederic Remington" paintings from the downstairs Old West–style barroom, "Rodin" drawings, and most of Pickfair's jade. ("Frederic Remington" and "Rodin" are in quotation marks because art experts said they weren't the real thing but rather copies of no great value.) Rogers said that he would put in his will that the artwork should go to the University of Southern California.

James Goodman, the man operating the auction, said, "This is the ultimate Hollywood house and I believe people will be buying as much for memory and legend as for investment." This probably was what Pickford had envisioned when drawing up her will.

As for the Pickfair property, it was sold in 1988 for $7 million to businessman Meshulam Riklis and his actress wife, Pia Zadora, who demolished the house and built a mansion on the site, which was then sold to a tech company that used it for events. Meanwhile, Buddy Rogers and new wife Beverly Ricono divided their time between Pickfair Lodge and a second home in Rancho Mirage, a desert resort near Palm Springs popular with the rich and famous, including many from the entertainment world. Following Buddy's death in 1999, Beverly sold Pickfair Lodge for $4 million in 2002.

Mary and Buddy's Oscars, however, continued to generate drama. Mary Pickford won her first Oscar, for best actress, in 1930 and a second, an honorary Oscar, in 1976 for "her contributions to American cinema." Buddy received his Oscar in 1986 in conjunction with receiving the Academy's Jean Hersholt Award for "outstanding contributions to humanitarian causes." Buddy and Beverly had kept all three Oscars in their Rancho Mirage home.

When Beverly died in 2007, her handwritten will instructed that Mary's best actress Oscar be auctioned off, with the proceeds to benefit the Buddy and Beverly Rogers Foundation and the Buddy Rogers Symphony for Young Musicians in Palm Springs. Mary's honorary Oscar and Buddy's Oscar were designated for Beverly's nieces, cousins Virginia Casey and Kim Boyer.

The Academy of Motion Pictures and Sciences (AMPAS) protested that such a sale would be in violation of its Oscar ownership rules. Starting in 1951, AMPAS has required recipients of its coveted golden statuettes to sign an agreement during the Oscars ceremony, immediately after accepting the prize, that gives the Academy first dibs to buy back the statuette should the winner, or their heirs, choose to get rid of it. The original token payment of $10 was subsequently reduced to $1. The Academy's objective, it says, is for "the Oscar to be treated with dignity, not as an item for sale to the highest bidder."

The acquisition of pre-1951 Oscars became in demand with people who could afford the steep prices. To sellers who preferred cash to sentiment, the hundreds of thousands of dollars they could make in the marketplace was far better than $1 from the Academy. Because Pickford signed the agreement when her honorary Oscar was presented to her and because she was a founder of the academy who remained a member until her death, academy officials contended that her 1930 best actress Oscar came under the rule on right of first refusal.

Beverly had named nieces Virginia Casey and Kim Boyer and Kim's mother, Marian Stahl, executors of her estate. Given the hot market for pre-1951 Oscars, Kim calculated that Mary's 1930 Oscar would fetch between $500,000 and $800,000 at auction. She told the Academy that to get the Oscar it would have to contribute $500,000 to Beverly's favourite cause, the Buddy Rogers Youth Symphony.

The Academy countered by offering to donate $25,000 a year for two years to the symphony. It said it wanted both of Mary's Oscars plus Buddy's.

When Boyer and Casey rejected this proposal, the Academy upped its offer to $200,000. "Only because Mary Pickford was a founder of the Academy," the Academy's legal counsel David Quinto said. Boyer and Casey rejected this offer, too, saying they wanted the Academy to donate $25,000 per year over eighteen years. Fed up with the haggling, the Academy said it would no longer negotiate, its $200,000 offer was "off the table," and it would take legal action. "And sure enough, we were hit with a lawsuit," Boyer said. It was filed in August 2007. "We are seeking to prevent the sale of all three statuettes," said Leslie Unger, director of communications for the Academy. "We are seeking a declaration from the court that all three of those statuettes are bound by our winner's agreement and therefore cannot be sold without providing the academy with first right of refusal."

A Los Angeles judge referred the matter to mediation, giving both sides a year, until August 2008, to resolve the dispute. If not, it would go to trial.

Boyer said she was particularly stung by the suit's allegation that the family intended to put all three Oscars up for sale. "We have never, ever discussed selling Buddy's or Mary's later Oscars," she said, adding, "We would never want to sell them."

"Virginia's family will be receiving one of them, and my family the other," said Boyer, who quit her secretarial job in Washington state's Snohomish school district, "to devote my time to the handling of my aunt's estate." She added: "We cherish and treasure them and feel humbled that we inherited them."

"We talked about it all the time, and my aunt said, 'These are going to stay in the family,'" Casey said.

Casey recalled that the Oscars stood on Beverly's baby grand piano and Beverly would encourage her to pick one up and have a maid snap a photo. "I'd hold it up, smile, and say, 'I'd like to thank all the little people who made this possible.' It was all lighthearted. We always had awe of them and total respect."

The cousins put Pickford's 1976 honorary Oscar on display in the "Mary Pickford Museum," a grandiose name for a small space in the lobby of the Mary Pickford Theater, a movie house named in her honour in Cathedral City between Palm Springs and Rancho Mirage. The theatre opened in 2001, and Beverly Ricono Rogers had been influential in its construction. "And where are the other two?" Kim Boyer was asked by the press. "In a very safe place," Boyer said, coyly adding, "I won't say where."

Casey and Boyer's attorney, Mark Passin, said, "The Academy has made it loud and clear they will spend a fortune — and we have to spend a fortune — on legal costs and not give the money to charity," he said.

"Mary Pickford was a founder of the Academy and one of the people who voted to approve the design of the Oscar," Academy lawyer David Quinto said. "Clearly, her Oscar should be returned."

On December 15, 2008, a Los Angeles jury, in an eleven-to-one verdict reached in just an hour, ruled that all three Oscars should go to the Academy.

Mary had been a combination of softness and steel in life, and her will was the same mixture, reflecting her oft-expressed belief: "If you have made mistakes, even serious mistakes, you may have a fresh start any moment you choose, for this thing we call 'failure' is not the falling down, but the staying down. The past cannot be changed. The future is yet in your power."

4

WILL OF INSULTS

> Being in sound health of body, and my mind just as usual (which my friends who flatter me say is no great shakes at the best of times), do make this my last will and testament....
>
> — WILLIAM DUNLOP

So begins the will of William "Tiger" Dunlop, one of the founders of Goderich, Ontario. A childless bachelor, Dunlop died on June 29, 1848, at age fifty-five. He left behind a unique will of comic (to him) insults that is still a classic quoted worldwide. It was one more eccentricity from a man who had happily lived his life as an eccentric.

Born in Greenock, Scotland, in 1793, the son of a banker, William Dunlop had many careers. A graduate in medicine from the University of Edinburgh, his first job was as a British Army surgeon, serving in America during the War of 1812. He then accompanied his regiment to India, where he went his own way, becoming a newspaper editor and, when he ran out of money, agreeing to lay the groundwork for a proposed colony for a land development company. The company sent him to reconnoitre an island off the coast of India, but when he arrived, totally on his own, he found that the island was a jungle filled with tigers. The nickname "Tiger" came from Dunlop's tale of killing many tigers that came around his tent, blinding them by throwing snuff at their eyes, then dispatching them with a single gunshot or a single thrust of his sword. Well, that was his claim.

After contracting malaria and recovering back home in Scotland, Dunlop's "next move was a characteristically eccentric one," essayist William Rattray wrote in volume two of his four-volume book *The Scot in British North America*, published in 1881. "He delivered a course of lectures on medical jurisprudence at the University of Edinburgh, described as a mixture of 'fun and learning, law and science, blended with rough jokes and anecdotes, not at all of the prudish nature.'" He then went to London and dabbled in journalism and became the secretary of a saltworks company near London. Rattray stressed that Dunlop was "a strictly honest fellow in every sense of the word and made nothing from the stock market bubbles of the time."

Dunlop came to Upper Canada (now Ontario) in 1826 as a scout for a British land development company interested in opportunities in southwestern Ontario. He helped establish the communities of Galt and Goderich. He also wrote for British magazines — one of his articles was memorably titled "The Autobiography of a Rat" — and Canadian literary and political magazines. In 1836 he helped found the Toronto Literary Club, where he frequently lectured.

During the 1837–38 Upper Canada Rebellion, he organized a ragtag militia unit, which he nicknamed "The Bloody Useless." When the unit ran short of supplies and food, he went to military headquarters and, to get what he wanted, said he was a general.

He was elected to the Union Parliament formed in 1840 when Upper and Lower Canada united and served until 1846 when he resigned. Rattray wrote: "He was a general favourite, partly on account of his well-known eccentricity, and partly from the racy character of his speeches. He was a forcible, but scarcely an eloquent, speaker, yet no sooner was he expected to speak than the House filled at once." An example of his wit: When a fellow member interrupted him as he spoke on the subject of taxation to ask him how he would like a tax on bachelors, he replied, "Admirably, luxury is always a legitimate object of taxation."

Dunlop and his brother Robert, a retired British Navy captain nicknamed "Robin," lived in a log cabin on a Goderich hilltop overlooking the harbour. They called their property and their home "Gairbraid," after the house their mother had grown up in Scotland and where they had been born. Informally, Tiger called it "The Castle." Though diametrically opposite in appearance and personality, the two brothers had been close since childhood. William was tall and broad, with flaming red hair. He had a booming voice and hearty laugh, dominated conversations, and was an enthusiastic practical joker. Robert was of average height, slim, brown-haired, quiet, soft-spoken, and self-effacing, and he didn't commit practical jokes. He was limited in activity because of a limp and a disabled hand from a war injury.

The brothers had a housekeeper, Louisa McColl. "They were compelled either to borrow money, or what was much the same thing, to go in arrears in payment of her wages, in order to tide them over an emergency," Rattray wrote. "It was found, on an examination of the accounts, that they were hopelessly in her debt; the doctor [William], therefore, startled his brother by stating that the only way to get out of the difficulty was for one or other of them to marry her."

So, with a coin toss, the brothers decided who would marry the housekeeper. William, who didn't want to ever marry, rigged the contest with a coin that had two heads. Louisa expressed no objection to marrying Robin, and the nuptials rapidly took place. William continued to live at Gairbraid with the couple, and Louisa continued to serve as housekeeper for the two brothers. When Robert died in 1841, Louisa remained, professedly as housekeeper.

William, a.k.a. "Tiger," a.k.a. "the Doctor," did everything on a grand scale, whether it be telling tall tales, flouting authority, entertaining, drinking, or taking snuff. The Dunlops frequently entertained guests at Gairbraid, with twelve, sometimes as many as twenty, crowded around the table — all of them men. The meal was conducted with great formality. The table was covered with a fine tablecloth and laid with elegant silverware, glassware, and chinaware. A major-domo, wearing a white coat, directed maids in bringing in and removing plates.

Dinner over, the table cleared, Louisa would depart from the room and the revelry would begin. A shiny brass toddy kettle (for warming spirits), with a container beneath it holding a red-hot iron, would be brought in. On a square embroidered doily was placed a silver toddy ladle, a saucer of sliced lemon, and a spice container with whole spices. Then Tiger rolled out what he called "The Twelve Apostles." This was a stout pine box, two feet square, mounted on casters, its inside lined with green felt to hold twelve one-gallon bottles. The twelfth held water when its owner was travelling; he referred to it as "Judas." Closed, the box held contents so firmly that they could even withstand a wagon trip over Canada's then-rutted, bumpy, pot-holed, dirt "roads." Open, it was easily wheeled on its casters around the dining room as the occupants sat in a semi-circle in front of a fireplace.

Although William wasn't much of a churchgoer — he proffered "three good reasons for why a person shouldn't attend church: First that a man should be sure to find his wife there, secondly, he could not bear any meeting where one man engrossed the whole of the conversation, and thirdly, that he never liked singing without drinking" — the local reverend was a frequent guest at Gairbraid and an enthusiastic imbiber. As the story goes, toward the end of an evening with The Twelve Apostles, the reverend slipped from his chair onto the floor. As a practical joke, Tiger and the others laid the man out flat on the floor, placed a sheet over him and a plate of salt on his chest, and lit candles at his head and feet. They put pennies on his eyelids and gathered about him in feigned sadness. The pennies slid off as his eyes opened. Tiger then conducted obsequies for "the Honourable, the very Reverend and Very Drunken...."

Tiger's consumption of snuff, which he kept in an immense box he called "the coffin," was gargantuan. When an American border inspector doubted that the quantity of snuff he was carrying could be simply for personal use, Dunlop tossed a handful into the air and snorted it up as it fell about him, saying, "There, that's what I want it for; that's the way I use it."

At a local general store in Goderich, he hid a live porcupine in a barrel that usually contained nails, then watched gleefully as unsuspecting shoppers stuck their hands inside. He delighted in dressing the part of an uncouth backwoodsman, and then surprising onlookers with a learned monologue.

Once, travelling in the bush with a logging chain wrapped about himself, he met an old friend from Scotland. When they parted, Dunlop asked the fellow to tell his friends at home that he had been found "in chains but well and happy."

Robin's death, followed by that of a beloved aunt, prompted Tiger to realize his own mortality, which led to his decision to write a will. He didn't want it to be earnest as wills typically are; rather, he wanted to be typically high-spirited.

On August 31, 1841, he asked the local magistrate to come to Gairbraid. On his arrival Tiger requested him to sit at his desk in the big dining room for the purpose of officially recording Tiger's last will and testament. After the two men quaffed a tankard of beer, Tiger dictated as the magistrate wrote in elegant, easy-to-read copperplate calligraphic script in back ink, straight lines on unruled paper, the same amount of space between all the lines:

> In the name of God Amen
> I William Dunlop of Gairbraid in the Township of Colborne County and District of Huron Western Canada Esquire being in sound health of body and my mind (which my friends who flatter me say is no great shakes at the best of times) do make this my last will and testament as follows revoking of course all former Wills.
>
> I leave the property of Gairbraid, and all other landed property I may be possessed of, to my sisters Helen Boyle Story and Elizabeth Boyle Dunlop, the former because she is married to a minister who (God help him) she hen pecks. The latter because she is married to nobody, nor is she like to be, for she is an old maid, and not market-rife, and also, I leave to them and their heirs my share of the stock and implements on the farm; provided always that the enclosure round my brother's grave be reserved, and if either should die without issue, then the other to inherit the whole.

I leave to my sister-in-law Louisa Dunlop all my share of the household furniture and such traps with the exceptions hereinafter mentioned.

I leave my silver tankard to the eldest son of Old John as the representative of the family. I would have left it to Old John himself, but he would melt it down to make medals and that would be sacrilege — however, I leave my big horn snuff box to him; he can only make temperance horn spoons of that.

I leave my sister Jenny my Bible, the property formerly of my great-great-grandmother, Bethia Hamilton of Wood Hall; and when she knows as much of the spirit of it as she does of the letter, she will be another guise Christian than she is.

I also leave my brother's watch to my brother Sandy, exhorting him at the same time to give up Whiggery, Radicalism, and all the other sins that do most easily beset him.

I leave my brother Alan my big silver snuff box as I am informed he is rather a decent Christian, with a swag belly and a jolly face.

I leave Parson Chevasse (Magg's husband) the snuff box I got from the Sarnia Militia, as a small token of my gratitude for the services he has done the family in taking a sister that no man of taste would have taken.

I leave John Caddle a silver teapot, to the end that he drink Tea therefrom to comfort him under the affliction of a slatternly wife.

I leave my books to my brother Andrew, because he has been so long a Jungley Wallah, that he may learn to read with them.

I give my silver cup, with a Sovereign in it, to my sister Janet Graham Dunlop because she is an old maid and pious, and therefore will necessarily take to horning, and

> also, my Gramma's snuff mull, as it looks decent to see an old woman taking Snuff.
>
> I do hereby constitute and appoint John Dunlop Esq of Gairbraid, Alexander Dunlop Esquire, advocate Edinburgh, Alan C. Dunlop Esquire, and William Chalk of Tuckersmith, William Stewart and William Gooding Esquires Goderich, to be the executors of this my last will and testament. In witness whereof I have set my hand and seal the Thirty-first of August in the year of our Lord One thousand eight hundred and forty-two.
>
> W Dunlop

The will completed, William and the magistrate quaffed more beer, then, chuckling, strode into the kitchen where Louisa and her two sisters and two brothers were gathered to escape the outdoor heat, drinking beers and chatting. William read aloud his magnum opus. They were both scandalized and amused.

Despite all his joking around, William was not without a heart. On February 14, 1845, he wrote a one-page codicil. It was straightforward, solemn, without even a speck of humour. It said:

> This is a codicil to my will already made. Notwithstanding any other devise contained in my will already made and executed, I hereby give and devise unto my good friend and sister-in-law Louisa Dunlop (widow of my late brother, Captain R.G. Graham Dunlop, of the Royal Navy) all that my dwelling house and garden with the close piece, or parcel of meadow or pasture land around and adjoining thereto and other appurtenances to the said house belonging.

Dr. William "Tiger" Dunlop died June 29, 1848, having never changed his will written six years earlier. Local MPP and lawyer John Prince, one of the witnesses of the codicil, submitted it and the will for probate November 22, 1848, having added at the bottom of the will, after the witnesses' signatures:

> I have perused the above will. It is eccentric, but it is not, on that score, illegal or informal. To a mind who knows the mind of the Testator it will remain a relic of his perfect indifference (an indifference to be admired, in my opinion) to what is called "Fashion" over one's testamentary.
>
> I conceive it to be a just and a proper will and no person can question its legality in point of form.

The probate court made no objections.

5

THE GREAT STORK DERBY WILL

> This Will is necessarily uncommon and capricious because I have no dependents or near relations and no duty rests upon me to leave any property at my death and what I do leave is proof of my folly in gathering and retaining more than I required in my lifetime.
>
> — CHARLES VANCE MILLAR

Charles "Charlie" Vance Millar was a wealthy Toronto lawyer, financier, champion racehorse owner, and notorious practical joker who died on October 31, 1926, at the age of seventy-two. The most "uncommon, capricious" clause of his will left the bulk of his estate to "the Mother who has in the ten years after my death given birth in Toronto to the greatest number of children."

Sparking what the press called "The Great Stork Derby," the clause enraged many, who claimed that it promoted "unbridled breeding with no regard to the well-being of the contestants and the children they bore." Numerous court challenges arose by people who popped up claiming they were relatives of the unmarried and childless Millar and therefore should get chunks of his estate.

Why would Charlie create such an uproar? A distant relative left a comment on the Find a Grave website, which suggests there was more to Charlie than just being a practical joker:

> Having a low opinion of human nature and a belief that everyone had a price, he [Charlie Millar] set out to prove his point. He skewered politicians, clergy, friends, enemies, piety and pomposity and provided comic relief during the most dreary years of the 1930s. He caused the country to examine attitudes towards sex, birth control, women's rights, religion, welfare, horseracing and prohibition, testamentary capacity, and testamentary freedom, and, as he crudely promised a friend prior to his death, made "****ing the most popular pastime in Toronto." The will and the chain of events following generated more copy on the front pages of the Toronto newspapers than any other single story in that entire decade.

Charlie Millar was born in the small southwestern Ontario town of Aylmer on June 28, 1854, the only child of well-known local farmer Simon Miller and his wife Sarah. As an adult, Charlie changed the *e* in his surname to an *a*, an example of his lifetime habit of going against convention. He excelled at school, averaging 98 percent in every subject at the University of Toronto and winning a gold medal for excellence in his graduating year before going on to attend Osgoode Hall Law School and graduating with high marks in 1881.

With his top academic results, Charlie should have been in high demand at the city's blue-chip law firms but being from the country he lacked establishment contacts. He was eventually taken on by a firm that took advantage of his having no other prospects, paying him a measly $3 a week. He must have pondered: "How can I afford both a place to live and food to eat?" A room in a low-price boarding house in Toronto then cost 35 cents a night, $2.45 a week. That left him with very little money to pay for food.

This hand-to-mouth existence went on for three years. Then, out of the blue, he had a break. He was befriended by Thomas McGaw, co-owner of the Queen's Hotel, then Toronto's most fashionable hotel, located downtown at the northeast corner of Front and Yonge streets. McGaw provided him room and board on credit, as well as giving him all the hotel's legal business and referring hotel guests in search of a lawyer to him. This enabled Millar to set up his own law practice. He never forgot McGaw's kindness. For twenty-three years, long after he became a prosperous lawyer and owner of half-a-dozen rental properties in downtown Toronto, he continued to live in a single room at the hotel.

The Queen's Hotel became the site from which he pulled his favourite practical joke, a kind of social behaviour experiment, year after year. He would surreptitiously place a dollar bill on the sidewalk in front of the hotel or on the handrail of the steps leading up to the entrance, sit in a chair on the hotel's front veranda, and time how long it took for someone to furtively scoop up the bill. Invariably, the dollar bill was quickly picked up, following which Millar replaced it with another. He liked to say that expensively dressed people snatched up the money with the same or even greater enthusiasm as shabbily dressed passersby. "There's nothing like money to show you a man's character," Charlie would say. He was referring to the bill grabbers, but the same words could be applied to him. "If you ever want to see a picture of guilt, just watch an honest man pocketing a dollar he has found," he said.

Although Millar had a successful corporate law practice specializing in contracts, most of his wealth was derived primarily from astute business investments. He was co-owner of the British Columbia Express Company, a mail, passenger, and freight company that used stagecoaches and paddlewheel steamships to get around the province; part owner of O'Keefe Ltd., the parent company of O'Keefe Brewery, Toronto; a major shareholder in a bonanza silver mine in northern Ontario nicknamed "The Silver Sidewalk," a fourteen-inch-wide strip of a huge amount of extractable silver ore; and co-founder and co-owner of Kenilworth Park Racetrack in Windsor, Ontario. A $2 purchase of Detroit River water lots, in anticipation of an underwater tunnel being constructed linking the Canadian and U.S. sides of the border from Windsor, Ontario, to Detroit, Michigan, proved its worth when construction began two years after his demise. The $2, a casual investment by Millar, became worth $100,000 ($1.7 million today), a major factor in the big increase in the value of his estate in the ten years after his death.

Charlie liked doing things himself rather than paying others. He learned carpentry and spent evenings after work repairing what was needed in his rental properties in Toronto.

He owned excellent racehorses, including Tartarean, 1915 winner of Canada's most prestigious annual horse race, the King's Plate, run in Toronto. The year after his death, Troutlet, a horse he had owned, won the 1927 King's Plate.

In 1903 he left the Queen's Hotel. After briefly renting a house near the University of Toronto, and then one in the city's well-to-do Rosedale neighbourhood, he had a mansion built on a double lot at the Scarborough Bluffs in Toronto's east side into which he moved in 1911 and lived until his death in 1926. He also had a vacation home in Jamaica. He drank alcohol sparingly, one glass at dinner, and went to bed every night at 9:00 p.m.

His eccentricities extended beyond changing *e* to *a* in his surname and dropping money and watching others scoop it up; he liked to sleep on the veranda outside his Scarborough home regardless of weather, including in winter. "It makes me tougher," he explained.

It was rumoured that in his younger days Charlie proposed to a young woman who accepted his offer of marriage but that her father said no because Charlie was poor at the time. He never did marry. Following the death of his own father in May 1901, Charlie's widowed mother moved in with him and lived with him until her death in October 1917. At the time of Charlie's death, a young law student named Charles H. Kemp, a farm boy who'd come to Toronto to get his degree as had Millar, was also living at Millar's home. There never was talk that their relationship was anything other than Millar befriending Kemp, paying it forward so to speak for Thomas McGaw having assisted him. That, however, was the extent of Millar's contributions to charitable causes in his lifetime.

On October 31, 1926, the day of his death, Millar finished a substantial lunch at the Queen's Hotel and walked a short block north to his office in the Crown Life Building at the corner of Yonge and Colborne streets in downtown Toronto's financial district to catch up on some work. It was a Sunday, which meant that the building's elevator was out of service due to it being the Sabbath. After climbing the three flights of stairs to his office, Charlie suffered a heart attack at his desk. He was pronounced dead at 4:30 p.m.

Millar was given respectful obituaries in Toronto newspapers, and *The New York Times* also noted his passing. His hometown newspaper, *The Aylmer Express*, praised him as being "a lawyer of the foremost rank and a man of sound judgment in business affairs." More than fifty prominent Torontonians attended his funeral service, which was held in his large Scarborough house, crammed with dozens of floral tributes. The presiding minister spoke in glowing terms about the deceased. Charles Millar was buried at the Burdick Cemetery on the outskirts of Aylmer, his birthplace, alongside his parents in a family plot.

Millar had drawn up his will five years earlier, on June 7, 1921, and named as executors James Lang, estates manager at Toronto General Trusts Corporation; Howard Vernon Hearst, estates manager at National Trust Company; and George Roy Sproat, his accountant for many years. Probate of his estate described his "property" as follows: household goods and furniture, $800; bank debts and promissory notes, $1,000; moneys secured by mortgage, $76,391.67; bank stock and other stocks, $125,490.53; one-half interest in five racehorses, $2,000; interest in law firm Millar & Hunter, $2,000; and real estate, $114,627.00, for a total value of $322,509.20 (about $5.5 million today).

On December 3, a few days before the will would be submitted for probate to the Ontario Surrogate Court, which processed probate applications, the first in a lengthy stream of objections to the contents of his will arose. Clause 5 of the will was leaked to the press by an unidentified source. It read: "At the death of Major Joseph Kilgour, I give to the Head Bishop of the Roman Catholic Church at Toronto five hundred dollars for Masses for the soul of the said Major as he will be greatly in need of help at that time."

The wording of the clause was deliberately and maliciously intended to convey the impression that Major Joseph Kilgour was a scoundrel, when in fact, he wasn't. Kilgour was a well-respected and influential businessman who had founded a successful company that produced cardboard boxes and paper grocery bags. He'd also transformed two hundred acres of scrub land near Toronto's then northern city limit into a working farm, "Sunnybrook Farm," where he and his wife, Alice, hosted fox hunts and horse-jumping competitions. (After his death she donated much of the property to the city for a public park, "Sunnybrook Park," one of Toronto's largest public spaces.) Kilgour died almost two years before Millar, but Millar had targeted him in his will because Kilgour's horses had often defeated his own at the racetracks. It would not be the only petty beef that would be revealed when the will was made public.

The head bishop of the Roman Catholic archdiocese of Toronto, Archbishop (Neil) McNeil, was also deeply offended by clause 5, having construed it as inferring that he could be bought (which was representative of Millar's jaundiced view that everyone could be). Upon reading the papers, the archbishop summoned Andrew Hunter, Millar's law partner, to his residence on Wellesley Place, a short street of fine homes in central Toronto, and insisted that the clause be expunged before the will was submitted for probate. Hunter said he would see to it that very day. He spoke to the will's three executors, and they immediately agreed to apply to the Surrogate Court to expunge the clause. When the document was submitted for probate two days later, Surrogate Court Judge Emerson Coatsworth gave written approval to excise the clause, and it was pasted over with a blank piece of paper in the letters probate that were issued.

One of the first indications of Millar's intent with his will when the letters probate were issued could be seen by the contrarian tone in the preamble:

> This Will is necessarily *uncommon* and *capricious* because I have no dependents or near relations and no duty rests upon me to leave any property at my death and what I do leave is proof of my folly in gathering and retaining more than I required in my lifetime.

In the first clause of the will, he wrote: "To A.L. Gourlay of the J.J. McLaughlin Company, Toronto, I give ten thousand dollars as he lost approximately that sum in a business transaction with me."

A.L. (Arthur Leslie) Gourley worked for the J.J. McLaughlin Company, most known as the creator of Canada Dry ginger ale. Millar misspelled Gourley's surname in his will; the correct spelling was "Gourley" (*e* not *a*). This was slightly surprising because, as a lawyer, Millar would have known the importance of correct spelling in a document; moreover, he'd had a reputation for meticulousness in the legal matters he handled. However, a typo or spelling error usually doesn't invalidate a will, the key issue being whether the court can discern the true intention of the testator.

What was Millar's true intention with this clause? He was again being nasty and petty; he had made Gourley wait to be reimbursed until after he died, when Millar very well could have paid him while alive. Gourley told the press: "I befriended Mr. Millar in a certain deal and as a result he reaped a substantial pecuniary advantage. I do not wish to detail to you the particulars of the transaction which resulted in the legacy. They are not of public interest." Perhaps Millar felt bad for taking so much of Gourley's cash … but not bad enough to pay him any of it earlier.

In clause 2, Millar willed $500 to his housekeeper, Mrs. Wilson. But as she predeceased Millar and he hadn't updated his will following her death, either through forgetfulness or slyness by him, the money became part of the residue, which would come to be known as the "Stork Derby Fund." Millar also left $1,000 to Charles Kemp, the young man living at his home.

Again, whether by oversight or not, clause 4 of Millar's will was also questionable. On the surface it seemed straightforward: "To Willis West of Edmonton I give one-half of the shares I own in the British Columbia Express Company."

Willis James West had worked for a Toronto law firm before moving to British Columbia in the early 1900s, where he became managing director of the British Columbia Express Company. In 1920 the company ceased operations in British Columbia and merged with the Lamson and Hubbard Canadian Company Limited, which was operating in Alberta, to become the Alberta and Arctic Transportation Company Limited, a one-thousand-mile steamer service between northern Alberta and the Northwest Territories, of which Charles Millar was president. By the time of Millar's passing, BC Express was defunct, and the 639 shares Millar still retained were worth only $2, which meant the value of West's legacy was a measly $1. Given his love of practical jokes, Millar may have been having fun at the expense of his business colleague. West probably didn't see any humour in Millar's stunt.

At this point when composing his will, Millar probably started to chuckle hard because he was about to embark on a series of practical jokes in the following clauses targeting members of the establishment whom he regarded as pompous and sanctimonious. While he worded the clauses in a non-joking manner, the humour for him was in what the impact would be on the recipients. In clause 6 he wrote:

> I give to Honourable W.E. Raney, A.M. Orpen and Reverend Samuel D. Chown, each one share in the Ontario Jockey Club providing three years from my death each one of them becomes enrolled as shareholders in the share register of the club and if they or any of them fail to do so the said three shares shall form part of my residuary estate.

Each share was worth $1,500. Millar had held four shares. The laugh for Millar was that he had paired Raney, an MPP, and Reverend Chown, both of whom were vociferous opponents of gambling, with Orpen, who owned gambling clubs and betting racetracks. One of the racetracks in which Orpen held an interest was Kenilworth Park Racetrack in Windsor, where Millar was a part owner. It turned out, however, that Millar had outsmarted himself and it was Rainey and Chown who had the last laugh. They spotted that Millar hadn't said they had to own their share in perpetuity, so they accepted, immediately sold, and contributed all the money to charity. Orpen was admitted as a member by the jockey club.

Clause 7 was a variation of expunged clause 5:

> To each duly ordained Minister of a Christian Church (except one Spracklin who shot a Hotelier) resident at my

> death in [the] Towns of Walkerville and Sandwich and the City of Windsor and earning an annual salary expounding the scripture to the sinners there, I give one share of the Kenilworth Jockey Club.

Sandwich and Walkerville, like Kenilworth, are Windsor suburbs. "Spracklin" was Reverend Joseph Oswald Lee Spracklin, a minister in Sandwich, a temperance zealot who'd doubled as a prohibition enforcement volunteer for the Ontario government since its implementation of prohibition in 1916. On November 3, 1920, Spracklin shot to death Beverley Trumble (who was a man — Beverley was a relatively common first name for a man at that time) at Trumble's roadhouse, which served liquor, during a raid. Spracklin was put on trial for manslaughter in February 1921, claimed Trumble was armed and that he had shot him in self-defence, and was acquitted. The case and the decision generated a lot of publicity and debate and would have been fresh in Millar's mind when he wrote his will in June 1921.

Of the other twenty-one clergymen in Windsor, Sandwich, and Walkerville, five accepted Millar's gift, only to discover that they were victims of a last laugh by Millar — one share was worth only half a cent! The track closed a few years later.

It's a puzzle as to why Millar picked on the clergy so much in his will. He set his sights on Protestant ministers and members of the Orange Lodge, a Protestant fraternal organization, in the next clause.

> To each Protestant minister exercising his clerical function at an annual salary and resident in Toronto at the time of my death and to each Orange Lodge in Toronto I give one share of the O'Keefe Brewery Company of Toronto, Limited.

This clause was a multi-part joke by Charlie. First, O'Keefe Brewery had been founded by a Catholic, Eugene O'Keefe. Second, Charlie owned only one share in O'Keefe Brewery. He did own substantial shares in its parent company O'Keefe Ltd., which is why he made certain to specify O'Keefe Brewery shares.

There were different interpretations of the motive for clause 9, which read,

> To T.P. Galt, K.C., J.D. Montgomery, and James Haverson, K.C., I give for life my house on Jamaica Island known as Ivy Green on the Half Way Tree Road and upon the death of the last survivor of them I direct my Executors and Trustees to sell the same and give the proceeds to the Council of the City of Kingston, Jamaica, for distribution among the poor of that City deserving help.

The press categorized it as a practical joke because "while Mr. Millar was friends with each, the three men are enemies who don't speak to one another." Legatee Montgomery, named in the will, said this was false. He gave this version: "Over dinner one night Charlie told me he intended to will the three of us Ivy Green. He said: 'Percy Galt, Jim Haverson, and you are three old crocks who should have your shoes torn off and be turned out to pasture. Ivy Green would be just the place for you.'" Whichever version was correct, the will didn't stipulate the three men had to stay in the house at the same time. But in the end, it didn't matter since Millar had sold the house three years after he wrote the will.

The three men weren't upset; all elderly, they said they were too old to travel anyway. If Millar had been serious about providing financial assistance to the "poor" of Kingston, Jamaica, he could have done it from the proceeds of his sale of Ivy Green in 1924. But his tight-fisted mantra was to never donate money to charitable causes.

Next in the will was clause 10, the bombshell that birthed The Great Stork Derby.

> All the rest and residue of my property wheresoever situate I give, devise, and bequeath unto my Executors and Trustees named below in Trust to convert into money as they deem advisable and invest all the money until the

> expiration of nine years from my death and then call in and convert it all into money and at the expiration of ten years from my death to give it and its accumulations to the Mother who has since my death given birth in Toronto to the greatest number of children as shown by the Registrations under the Vital Statistics Act. If one or more mothers have equal highest numbers of registrations under the said Act to divide the said moneys and accumulations equally between them.

Millar signed off with a clause naming his three trustees, which on the surface appeared dead serious but in fact was mean-spirited, Charlie's final laugh in his last-laugh will. The two trust companies he appointed were fierce competitors, and no doubt Millar would have nearly died laughing contemplating the stress working together likely would cause them.

When the will's quirky terms became public knowledge, people wondered, "Is this weird will legal? Was Charles Vance Millar of sound mind?" "Yes" and "Yes," the court declared.

Clause 10, the baby race, caused the most debate and controversy. Was it "testamentary freedom" or was it against public policy (the public good) because it encouraged what opponents charged was "unbridled breeding with no regard to the well-being of the contestants and the children they bore"? Especially since Canada's infant mortality and maternal childbirth death rates were very high back then.

Famous birth control advocate Margaret Sanger was outraged, saying, "It reduces woman to an animal and is deplorable." Ontario Premier Mitchell Hepburn called it "the most revolting and disgusting exhibition ever put on in a civilized country." His government introduced legislation to redirect the money to the University of Toronto, Millar's alma mater, claiming that was his original intention. But following objections to the government butting into personal decisions, the bill was hastily withdrawn.

Other critics said the money should have been earmarked for orphanages, open-air nurseries, and support for the "Drink Milk" campaign under way to eradicate rickets, a serious health problem then among children that deforms bones partly caused by the lack of bone-strengthening milk consumption.

For the stork derby contenders, however, the contest seemed a lifeline. The families were all poor, and the Great Depression, which began a couple of years after Millar's death, made their situation even more dire. By contest's end — October 31, 1936, at precisely 4:30 p.m., ten years on the dot from Millar's death — the value of the prize had risen to $568,106 (more than $12 million today). During this time the contestants had had many children, one as many as thirteen. They seem not to have taken into consideration that if they lost, they'd be on their own in having to provide for a large brood of children.

Millar had defenders. They included John Montgomery, one of the three men to whom he'd bequeathed his Jamaica home. "Charlie Millar was one of the finest chaps I ever knew. He wasn't a crank or an eccentric, but an individual," Montgomery said. "No one can ever say Charlie Millar did a mean thing."

"It was his money and he could do as he darn pleased with it."

John Bruce, another friend of Millar, said: "The will is a great lesson against a 'holier than thou' attitude." The stork derby clause was well intentioned, he said: "He was trying to shame the government into legalizing birth control." If so, it was an extreme way to do it.

Abe Orpen, bequeathed one of Millar's Ontario Jockey Club shares, said, "He was likable but hard-boiled. Charlie was very sparing in his charity. He was a very close man — a close-fisted man.

"About this will of his, I believe the only reason Millar didn't include the fathers was because he thought there wouldn't be enough money to divide among the winners."

In addition to public debates, the will also sparked legal battles over the stork derby clause, some by women participating in the contest and some by Americans claiming to be Charlie's cousins. This created an unexpected windfall for the law profession; twenty-eight lawyers in total were hired. It was welcome income during the depression when clients were few and far between.

The distant cousins — they conceded they were not close relations — applied for the will to be declared invalid on the grounds that the stork derby clause was against public policy. If such an application was approved, Millar would have been said to have died "intestate," "not having made a will," and the estate's assets under the law would be divvied out to next of kin, which was what the pop-up relatives were characterizing themselves as.

The case was overseen by William Edward Middleton, chief justice of the Ontario Supreme Court. He ruled that the will was valid: "I regard the clause in question as prompted by sympathy for the mothers of large families, who are often extremely poor people, not unmingled with a queer sense of humour." The relatives went upward to the Ontario Court of Appeal. When it sided with Middleton, they went further up the judicial hierarchy to the Supreme Court of Canada. It dismissed the appeal at warp speed on December 22, 1936.

Globe and Mail reporter Harold Dingman wrote:

> The Supreme Court of Canada sat for exactly one minute today, but in that brief time raised the hopes of more than a dozen Toronto mothers for a share in the fortune left by Charles Vance Millar.
>
> Four of the judges filed into the dingy Supreme Court Chamber at five minutes past noon. Chief Justice Sir Lyman P. Duff announced: "The appeal is dismissed."
>
> The court immediately adjourned.
>
> The court's decision throws the question back to the Ontario courts, probably to Mr. Justice Middleton who will be called upon to decide which mother or mothers will get the money.

The people claiming to be relatives of Millar could have appealed the decision upward further to the United Kingdom Privy Council, which until 1949 was above the Supreme Court of Canada, but didn't, recognizing that their chances of success were nil.

The issue did return to Justice Middleton. "He has to be Solomon," *The Globe and Mail* said. Justice Middleton announced his decision March 19, 1938, sixteen months and two weeks after the contest closed. He ruled on three counts: whether stillborn, illegitimate, and children born just outside Toronto's city limits should be included. Middleton said no. Contestant Mrs. Lillian Kenny had included a stillborn child in her count, and contestant Mrs. Pauline Mae Clarke included five children who weren't fathered by her husband, including one born outside of Toronto.

Middleton declared a four-way tie between Annie Katherine Smith, Kathleen Ellen Nagle, Lucy Alice Timleck, and Isabel Mary Maclean, each of whom gave birth to nine children during the derby. Each received $110,000 (about $2.3 million today). *Time* magazine called it "The Fecundity Fortune." Lillian Kenny and Pauline Mae Clarke each received $12,500 (equivalent to $263,833 today) out of court in exchange for abandoning pending appeals.

The winnings were pared down to $75,000 by lawyer fees, court costs, and other expenses — still a nice golden egg, equivalent to $1.5 million today.

Millar's "stork derby" will clause wasn't a one-time phenomenon. There was a similar clause in the will of Thomas Foster, mayor of Toronto when Millar died, and his extraordinary will became public knowledge. Foster decided to emulate the clause, which people found out when he died on December 10, 1945, at the age of ninety-three.

> As I approve of large families as such and desire to extend some benefit to the mothers of such families, I direct my trustees to set aside a fund which, with interest, will provide the sum of $2,500 at the end of each of 4- to 10-year periods, the first commencing at my death, the second three years after my death, the third six years after my death and the fourth nine years after my death.
>
> The money is to be distributed among mothers living in Toronto for at least one year prior to the start of each period, who have given birth "in lawful wedlock to the children during the 10-year period in question." The mother giving birth to the largest number of children is to receive $1,250. Second prize is $800 and third prize is $450 in each of the four periods.

Foster, a self-made millionaire, the son of poor English immigrants, was worth $1,168,555 (about $20.5 million today) when he died. He was interred in a replica of India's magnificent Taj Mahal tomb he'd had constructed outside Toronto at a cost of $200,000 for his wife, who'd died in 1920, and their only child, Ruby, who died at the age of ten.

While the babies clause in his will echoed Millar's will, Foster otherwise was far different from Millar, the complete antithesis. There were no gibes, no mean-spirited bequests in his will, and he gave many charitable bequests, including money to charwomen working in downtown Toronto office buildings and newsboys. He also left money to feed the city's birds in winter, reward conscientious Bible class students, establish a flagpole at a high school, and provide for disabled patients at a hospital. His generosity continued with large sums for planting trees along Toronto streets and for cancer research. He also left money to relatives and gave a month's exemption from paying rent to tenants in his buildings.

There's no record of whether his stork derby will clause sparked a population boom as Millar's did.

6

DEAD HAND CONTROL

Imagine these scenarios: You've decided to go on a solitary sheer rock-face mountain climb, or deep-sea diving where sharks have been spotted, or paragliding, or trekking through a snake-and-tiger-filled jungle — none of which you've done before. Or maybe you've decided to go on a long voyage against doctor's orders. Or you've decided to enlist in the military. You say to yourself, "This is risky, dangerous, possibly fatal. Better write a will." Then, you think it over: You want to set restrictions; you only want the will to become effective if you die under these circumstances. You write: "If I die on this trip ..." or "If I die while on military duty...."

Or maybe you want to dictate or change the way a person is living their life: My grandson Jimmy must give up drinking and carousing / go to university / get top marks / become a doctor or lawyer / carry on the family business. My granddaughter Griselda must marry/divorce a person of this faith / ethnicity / sexual orientation / nationality. The bequest becomes void if the designated recipient doesn't conform to the decrees in the will.

The formal term for all of these types of wills is "conditional"; the colloquial terms are "dead hand control" and "ruling from the grave." The first type, in which the will comes into effect in the event of a specific circumstance, is known as a contingency will and usually isn't controversial. The second type, however — when the testator tries to control, like a puppet master or, put more crudely, like a meddlesome buttinsky, the actions of others — tends to be contested in court as inappropriate.

The following are notable Canadian examples of both types of conditional wills.

On the Battlefield

First, a poignant example of the contingency version. In case he died at Ypres, Belgium, where the fighting in the First World War between Canadian forces and German troops was particularly intense with many casualties on both sides, Thomas McKinnon, a twenty-year-old gunner in an ammunition column of Canada's Second Division, wrote a will in his paybook, carried in a pocket of his uniform. He died on June 24, 1916, of wounds suffered during battle. His pencilled will left his entire estate to his sister, Mrs. I. Mason, 2 Lewis Street, Toronto. It consisted of "cash in the bank $223 and $40 arrears of pay."

The probate court readily accepted the will as valid.

Risky Journey Will

Another distinctive Canadian conditional contingency will is that of Cornelius Rempel, a Manitoba Mennonite who died in 1921 at age sixty-five. Whether his will was valid or not went all the way up to Manitoba's Court of Appeal.

Cornelius was born on October 15, 1856, in Schoenhorst in Chortitza Colony, the first Mennonite colony in South Russia (now Ukraine), which was started in the late 1700s at the invitation of Russia's empress, Catherine the Great. She promised to respect the Mennonites' opposition to military service due to their pacifist beliefs and their customs in return for their applying their agrarian skills to turn the area into thriving farmland. Many Mennonites who had encountered hostility elsewhere in Europe because of their beliefs accepted the deal.

By the 1870s, however, the situation had changed. Russia's then-ruler, Tsar Alexander II, removed their military exemption and began to exert control over Mennonite schools and institutions. The Mennonites decided they had to leave and thought it best to depart Europe entirely. Their desire coincided with the Canadian government's desire to develop the West. To induce the Mennonites to come, the government promised them exemption from military service, religious freedom, their own school system, and grants of large tracts of land for their exclusive settlement. It made special amendments just for them to the Dominion Lands Act, allowing them to settle in groups in their usual cluster style, unlike the standard policy that each farmer had to reside upon his own homestead, a rule intended to spread settlement rapidly across the West.

Manitoba's government set up two "reserves" for Mennonites extending over fifty miles, one on the east side of the Red River and the other on the west side.

Cornelius Rempel, in his early twenties, was among the seven thousand Mennonites who moved to Manitoba from South Russia in the 1870s. Cornelius first lived in the Manitoba Mennonite community of Rosenort, in the north part of the Mennonites' sector. A few years later, on January 8, 1882, in Halbstadt, Manitoba, he married Anna Friesen, also a Mennonite, with whom he had a daughter. Sadly, Anna passed away not long after.

Cornelius remarried. He and his second wife, Katharina, had four children and lived in Blumenort, also in Mennonite territory. Per the Mennonite customs of the day, Cornelius and his sons would have dressed conservatively in a collarless shirt, a plain jacket and trousers, and a hat. His wife and daughters would have worn long, plain dresses and big bonnets, no makeup, and no jewellery. The Mennonites abstained from modern technology, travelling by horse and buggy rather than motorized vehicle when cars began to be manufactured, and had no electricity in their homes. The group was self-contained, self-reliant, and reclusive, with self-government, separate schools, communal shared resources and responsibilities, mutual aid, and own places of worship.

Manitoba's policy toward Mennonites changed regarding education with the passage in 1916 of the School Attendance Act, which said that if a private school didn't meet government-set standards, it would be closed and replaced with a public school that all children would have to attend. Saying that this edict contravened the 1873 federal government agreement that they could have their own educational system, the Mennonites continued to send their children to their own schools. The Manitoba government reacted by declaring these schools "unusable," fired and jailed the preacher-teachers, and made attendance at a public school compulsory.

The broken promise and once again persecution of their convictions prompted the group to look into migrating to a new place. Cornelius was in the forefront, selected as one of two Manitoba representatives on a six-person committee of community elders to scout for locations in Mexico. The committee members were heading into what for them was the unknown. All sorts of dangers could be lurking. Maybe they'd die.

In case he didn't return, Cornelius wrote a conditional will on January 26, 1921, a few days before departing for Mexico. It read:

> Whereas I am going to go on a journey to Mexico, and should I die, I therefore certify by these presents that my wife, Katharina Rempel is entitled to collect and draw all my outstanding monies, for which also Bank cheques are signed, as are in the Bergthaler Waisenamt, Altona, standing as deposits, and in the Bank of Hamilton, Gretna, standing as deposits, wheat tickets, and different outstanding monies according to book account also. She is consequently entitled to administer the whole estate and effects according to our Orphan Rules. For confirmation I sign this with the signature of my name.

The Bergthaler Waisenamt in Altona, a Mennonite hub in southern Manitoba, administered estates and also functioned as a Mennonite bank, accepting deposits and making loans to church members.

His affairs in order, Cornelius headed off for Mexico City with the other committee members. They safely arrived on February 16, 1921, and were received by Mexican president Álvaro Obregón. He agreed that the Mennonites could move in for the same reason Catherine the Great and the Canadian government previously had — the Mennonites' skill in turning dirt into arable land. He allocated them a portion of Chihuahua State, located in northern Mexico, bordering the U.S. states of New Mexico and Texas, on their pledge that they would transform the dry, sandy land into fertile farmland. The Mennonites agreed to buy 230,000 acres in Chihuahua at $8.25 an acre with a down payment of $2.25 each.

For his part, President Obregón signed a promissory "privilegium" that the Mennonites would have the "privileges" of exemption from military service, their own schools with no government interference, and religious freedom.

Satisfied, Cornelius and the rest of the delegation went home to seek approval for the deal. The *privilegium* was hailed as an answer to prayer, and Mennonites in Saskatchewan were invited to join in the move. But difficulties arose in both provinces in the sale of their farms, making immediate relocation impossible. Nevertheless, authorization was given for a delegation to go to Mexico in early September and finalize the transaction. Cornelius was a member of the group.

Just before leaving, he wrote:

> Gretna, Man.,
> Sept. 7th, 1921.
> To the Bergthaler Waisenamt, Altona.
> Confirm by these presents that you pay my deposit in full to my wife Katharina Rempel. Confirm above with signature of my name and witness.
> Witness, [Sgd.] F. Rempel [Sgd.] CORN. Rempel

Cornelius died on the way back in Minnesota, 440 miles south of the Manitoba border, on September 23, 1921, and his body was brought to Manitoba for burial.

When Cornelius's will was submitted to the Surrogate Court of the southern judicial district of Manitoba, the court said it was no longer acceptable because Cornelius had returned alive from his January trip.

Katharina, however, thought the will's opening sentence, "Whereas I am going on a trip to Mexico," meant that it applied to whenever her husband went to Mexico, and she filed an appeal with Manitoba's Court of Appeal. The case was heard May 18, 1922.

The court's chief justice, William Edgerton Perdue, delivered the court's unanimous decision in writing a month later. It was good news for Katharina. "Looking at the will in question in this appeal, I think it is clear that the contemplated journey to Mexico is referred to as a period of danger which operates as a reason why the testator should make his will. The operation of the will is not confined to that period."

In other words, "You're right, lady."

Who's the Boss?

The other category of conditional will is "in terrorem," Latin for "into / about fear." In this type of will, the beneficiary will lose all entitlement to the bequest if they don't adhere to the condition(s) set out by the testator. This tends to ignite battles over who the boss is over a bequest — the beneficiary or the deceased?

Such was the case involving the will of John Donald McBride, who died January 15, 1979. McBride sought to break up the marriage of his son, Robert, his only child, by means of his conditional will. He'd done his darndest to do this while alive, and having failed he opted to use his will as a weapon to posthumously get what he wanted and show that he was the boss. That's why his will said,

> Upon the death of my wife, if my son Robert McBride is married to Geraldine Elizabeth Gibbons, who formerly resided at 14 Cavell Avenue Mimico, to divide what then remains of my estate in equal shares among the Ontario Heart Foundation, Canadian Cancer Society, and Ontario Society for Crippled Children.
>
> But upon the death of my wife, if my son Robert McBride is not married to Geraldine Elizabeth Gibbons, to pay, transfer and convey all that remains of my estate unto my son, Robert McBride for his own use absolutely.

Robert and Geraldine had married on April 13, 1973, and were married when John executed his will on February 21, 1974, and still married — "happily," Robert said — at the time of John's death in 1979 and afterward.

Robert thought he should be the boss of his own life. He was very angry at his father for trying to rule his life from the grave with his will. He applied to what was then called the Ontario High Court of Justice, now the Ontario Superior Court, "to construe" the will. "To construe" means to determine the meaning of the text based on the rules of legal interpretation. The term can also be applied to government statutes, regulations, and court decisions.

Robert wanted to forestall the paragraphs controlling his marriage coming into effect when his mother, Millina, died. Millina was on Robert's side in the matter, not her dead husband's.

Robert submitted an affidavit that said, "I was married to Geraldine Elizabeth Gibbons at the time my father executed the will and he knew we were married when he did so." Robert went on to say that his father "always disliked my female companions and had been successful in breaking up relationships prior to my meeting Geraldine. We had an argument about Geraldine. I believe the two paragraphs were inserted in the will to cause me to leave my wife and that my father wanted to keep me in the family home to look after him and my mother before marrying."

Justice David Howard Woodhouse Henry construed the will in Robert's favour. In his January 28, 1980, opinion he said, "The charities were never intended to benefit except as a device to induce termination of the marriage. Therefore, Robert McBride will be entitled to the residue upon this mother's death regardless of whether he is or is not then married to Geraldine."

The lesson from this story? Love conquers all, even the attempted controlling hand of a parent after their death.

Antediluvian

Reverend Ambrose Ross Murley of Marystown, Newfoundland, self-described as a "retired United Church clergyman," was antediluvian in his views about religious faith and about the role of women. He disliked many types of Christianity, and he felt women were inferior to men. Believing his views were the proper views, and to enforce them after his death, he composed a number of do-it-my-way-or-you-get-nothing conditions in his will.

When he died in 1991 at age eighty-two, his chief heir, grandson Timothy Clarence Nelson Michael Murley, was just a baby, incapable of questioning the limits his grandfather's will would have on his life's direction.

The will bestowed on Timothy the dead man's home and its furnishings, nearby land on which he grew vegetables and collected wood, the money in his bank account, a 1973 Chevelle car, a Ford '82 Courier truck, and a gas and energy bond on the following condition:

> In order for Timothy Clarence N. Michael Murley to become heir to my Estate he must remain in one or the other main stream Christian Churches, that is, Roman Catholic, Anglican Church or the United Church of Canada or any name the latter Church may adopt. It is my last will and Testament that he never belong to such organizations as Pentecostals, Seventh Day Adventists, Jehovah Witnesses or Latter-Day Saints, so called. I make these rules following Old Testament holy men who ordered that their sons or relatives never become part of lesser religious organizations. I want him to be a real Christian.

Reverend Murley's other heir was his nephew Larry Gorden [*sic*] Murley, to whom he bequeathed ownership of a second house he owned in which Larry was living:

> But in case of a marriage failure or separation the house and land does not belong to him nor his wife to be sold and the money divided between the two potentially separating parties. It belongs to Larry's male, hopefully, successor, or to be owned jointly by Timothy Clarence N. Michael Murley in case of separation or divorce.

The will appointed Timothy's mother, Helen, executrix. She asked the Supreme Court of Newfoundland and Labrador for "interpretation of my late uncle's will so I may properly distribute the proceeds of the estate."

Justice David Riche of the Supreme Court of Newfoundland and Labrador — Trial Division released his decision on May 15, 1995, starting with the reverend's religion condition:

> I will deal with this first because it can be disposed of without lengthy reasoning. I am satisfied that such a provision which restricts the religious affiliation of any person is, in Canada, contrary to public policy.

In other words, Canada has freedom of religion. Justice Riche continued:

> Further, in this case, if it was not contrary to public policy, it would have to be declared void because the bequest could not take effect until the death of the beneficiary because only then one would know whether or not he had become associated with any religious group not approved of by the testator. In short, the gift could never be perfected.

As for the reverend's words "Larry's male, hopefully, successor," Justice Riche disposed of those too: "The words, 'hopefully male' is merely a wish and would have no effect, so that the successor could be either male or female."

The lesson from these stories is that whether conditional wills are obeyed depends on the circumstances.

7

FEUD

For two decades, a one-page will leaving an estate of $15 million, equivalent to half a billion dollars today, was feuded over by three generations of Dunsmuirs, British Columbia's wealthiest and most powerful family in the late 1800s and early 1900s. By the end the family was torn apart and its fortune and power gone.

There are, though, three visual reminders of the family today: Craigdarroch Castle, a thirty-nine-room mansion on a Victoria, British Columbia, hilltop commissioned by Robert Dunsmuir, founder of the family fortune, now a public tourist attraction; Hatley Castle in Victoria, built by Robert's eldest son, James, now the site of Royal Roads University; and the small northwest California town of Dunsmuir, named in honour of Robert's youngest son, Alexander, who donated money for a town-centre fountain on the proviso that the hitherto unnamed community be named after him.

Admired by some and hated by others, Robert Dunsmuir was a rags-to-riches success story. Robert was born in 1825 in Kilmarnock, southwest Scotland, a coal-mining district (and the birthplace of Johnnie Walker whisky), where he became a miner. In 1847 he married a local girl, Joan White, who gave birth just eight days after the nuptials to their first child,

Elizabeth. The couple was publicly rebuked by their church for "having antenuptial fornication" (the term then for premarital sex). In that era, particularly at Presbyterian churches in Scotland, "antenuptial fornication" was a serious offence subject to public penance, such as standing at the church door wearing sackcloth.

As a young man, Robert had a reputation as a heavy drinker who often had to be carried home from the local taverns. Although heavy drinking would become a lifelong habit, Robert always managed to be clear-headed in business.

In 1851, by which time the couple had had another daughter, Agnes, the family left for coal-rich Vancouver Island in search of new opportunities. A son, James (alternately called "Jim" or "Jamie"), was born during the voyage. Robert landed a job paying $5 a week as a coal digger at the coal division of the Hudson's Bay Company, the island's largest coal mines operator. Over the next eighteen years, he moved to a number of other coal mining companies on the Island. A second son, Alexander ("Alex"), was born in 1853, followed by five more daughters — Marion, Mary, Jessie, Emily, and Euphemia ("Effie").

Then in 1869, Robert, now forty-two years old, suddenly struck it rich by chance. As he told it, he was on his way back through the woods after fishing at a lake near Nanaimo, a coal centre on northeast Vancouver Island, when he tripped over what he first thought was a tree root but then realized was a coal seam. He staked a claim over a large surrounding area, calling what turned out to be a big coal bed the Wellington Mine. With his newfound enterprise Robert made a fortune, enabling him to build a multi-branch empire that encompassed every aspect of British Columbia's economy and gained him the nickname "King Grab." The empire included more collieries, a 68.5-mile railway he constructed connecting Nanaimo to Esquimalt Harbour at the southern tip of Vancouver Island, an ironworks, a dike-building company, steamships, a sawmill, a theatre, extensive real estate holdings, and a sandstone quarry, the source of the sandstone for the exterior of Craigdarroch Castle.

He relied a great deal on Joan's advice in building his empire. In effect she was his co-CEO. He called her "the backbone" of the family. Like Robert, she was tough as nails. They had one more child, their eighth, in 1872, a girl they named Maude. Robert was then forty-seven and Joan forty-four.

With wealth came power; Robert obtained a seat in the provincial legislature, where he made sure that any coal-mining legislation was favourable to him. It was said that he "carried the government in his breeches pocket."

It might be thought that with his own experience of being paid so little as a labourer he would be generous to his employees. Not so; instead he was cruel and paid his workers a pittance. Furthermore, the houses in the company towns he built at his mines were shanties for which he imposed astronomical rent. He threatened to evict workers if they went on strike for better pay and working conditions. An 1884 explosion at his Wellington Mine killed twenty-three people, and another in 1888 killed sixty.

The Dunsmuirs' eldest daughter, Elizabeth, married John Bryden, a man similar in background to Robert in that he had started as a coal digger. Over the years Bryden became a senior manager at a rival company to Robert's; Robert hired him away, the only son-in-law he employed. Second-oldest daughter Agnes married a shopkeeper.

As his wealth skyrocketed, Robert, in stark contrast to his tight-fistedness with his workers, spent big on himself and his family. He and Joan aspired to become part of high society. In 1885 they moved south from Nanaimo to the city of Victoria, British Columbia's legislative and social capital. Robert bought a large estate, Fairview, and at the time of his death was having the even grander Craigdarroch built.

In 1876, when he was twenty-five, eldest son James married Laura Miller Surler, a wealthy North Carolina belle to whom he'd been introduced by her brother, a mining engineering classmate at Virginia Agricultural and Mechanical College in Blacksburg, Virginia. Now known as Virginia Tech, the school was only in its fourth year in 1876 with just three instructors. James and Laura at first lived in Nanaimo, where James was put in charge of the family's coal interests there, then later in Victoria.

Second son Alexander was made the head of the company's San Francisco sales and shipping branch office. Away from immediate family oversight, he embarked on womanizing and heavy drinking. Robert always gave notice of his intention to visit to check up on the Frisco office, and Alexander would temporarily put his debauchery on hold. Nobody at the office clued Robert in about Alexander's party life. Alexander had inherited Robert's ability to be clear-headed in business despite excessive drinking away from work.

Once settled in Victoria, Robert and Joan embarked on a campaign to reel in pedigree young men to wed their six remaining unmarried daughters, a real-life version of the chase in the early nineteenth-century novels of Jane Austen for social standing through strategic matchmaking of daughters. Robert was typical of business tycoons of humble origin who bulldoze their way into high society by striking deals with indolent, impecunious bluebloods, particularly titled ones, in which the blueblood marries the tycoon's daughter in return for a luxurious lifestyle and the clearing away of debt. By 1889, the year Robert died, Marion, Mary, and Jessie had been married off.

The husbands were of varied calibre. Jessie snagged English-born Sir Richard Musgrave when he was visiting BC on one of his salmon fishing expeditions, a passion of his. Besides being titled he possessed an estate but had dissipated his money. Deeply in debt, he was happy that Jessie had come his way and would bail him out with Robert's money. Mary was betrothed to Henry Croft, owner of a sawmill in the Chemainus Valley on the east coast of southern Vancouver Island. He later ventured into copper mining and was a member of the provincial legislature from 1886 to 1894. All his business ventures went bust. Marion was affianced to Colonel Charles Frederick Houghton. When it was discovered on the brink of their wedding that he already had a wife and two children, Robert provided him with a big chunk of cash to ditch his family, which Houghton did.

The umbrella name for the business empire was Robert Dunsmuir & Sons, but Robert retained sole control with Joan the power behind the throne. Robert appointed James as manager of the company's operations in Departure Bay harbour, Nanaimo, only to demote and replace him with John Bryden, which was humiliating for James. Neither James nor Alex had shares, and they weren't paid regular salaries. Instead, Robert said, "Take what you want, just don't take too much." The brothers lived in comfort but were on a tight leash.

In early April 1889 Robert's health failed, his kidneys corroded from years of hard drinking. Lying in bed, barely conscious, on Wednesday, April 10, he asked the three doctors surrounding his bed, "Am I in danger? If so, I want to sign the will I recently wrote." Robert was referring to his second will that divided everything between James and Alexander. It had been prepared for some time, but he'd dithered over signing it, perhaps influenced by Joan, the sole beneficiary of his initial will. Robert dominated everyone in British Columbia save Joan, who was sitting at his bedside when he addressed the doctors.

The doctors evaded giving a straight answer. "There's no danger. You'll feel improved tomorrow," they assured him. Robert rallied a bit the next day but died the day after.

As soon as the funeral obsequies were over, the family gathered at Fairview to hear Robert's will. It was just one page and there was just one beneficiary. It read:

> I Robert Dunsmuir of Victoria in the Province of British Columbia Colliery Proprietor do hereby revoke all former wills and testamentary depositions made by me and declare this to be my last will and testament. Subject to the payment of all my just debts, funeral and testamentary expenses I give, devise and bequeath all my property — both real and personal — to my dear wife Joan Olive Dunsmuir absolutely and appoint her the sole executor of this my will. In witness whereof I have set my hand to this my will the twentieth day of January 1887.

It was extremely rare, and still is in large measure, for a man to entrust his widow with his entire estate. The standard procedure was and is to appoint advisory and supervisory outside trustees, usually from a trust company. For Robert to have left everything in Joan's hands was exceptional, a full expression of faith in her.

James and Alex were stunned and outraged. Sputtering with rage, they shouted in unison at their mother, "Father always led us to believe it was going to be us. There must be another, more recent will."

Joan, however, was icy calm; she held the winning hand. "Yes," she acknowledged, "there was another, newer will with the terms you were led to expect but Robert decided not to sign it. Instead, he chose to leave everything in my hands."

She proceeded to put them in their place. "I'll divide your father's corporate directorships between you but all the shares will be controlled by me. James, you'll get the title of president of the Wellington Colliery. You're to move from Nanaimo to here, Victoria, and you can sit in what was your father's headquarters office on Store Street. Alex, you'll get the title of president of the E & N [Esquimalt & Nanaimo Railway] and continue to be in San Francisco.

"You'll both report to me. I'm in charge.

"And by the way, no salaries for either of you, just as happened with your father." This meant that she now controlled their lives as Robert had.

She added salt to the wound. "I'm taking Emily, Effie, and Maude to England," she announced. "While I'm gone see to it that Craigdarroch is completed."

"We're doing all the work while you and they galivant on the money we make for the company," Jim and Alex complained. Joan ignored them. The purpose of the trip was to find husbands for her youngest daughters, still single.

There were mixed results. Captain Northing Pinckney Snowden of North Yorkshire, England, the man found for Emily, turned out to have syphilis, became insane, and had to be institutionalized. Effie wed Sir Somerset Arthur Gough-Calthorpe, a Royal Navy officer, the second titled peer obtained by the Dunsmuirs through marriage, the first being Jessica's Sir Richard Musgrave. Now they were Lady Jessica and Lady Euphemia, a big step up the social ladder for the family. Maude was married to Reggie Chaplin, an officer in the 10th Royal Hussars, also called the Prince of Wales's Own. He spent the money she brought to the marriage on playing polo. Joan threw extravagant weddings for all three girls, with each wearing a jewel-encrusted wedding gown. She thought she'd impressed blueblood high society back home in Victoria, but they derided her pretentiousness.

Joan returned home in September 1890, seventeen months after her departure, having waited until James and Alex had completed her assignment of getting Craigdarroch completed. They griped that she had greatly overspent when away. She paid no attention.

Over the following years the brothers pestered Joan to give them more than what they regarded as crumbs. By 1896 they had worn her down. She was now sixty-eight. She handed over much of the empire to them, with the exception of the crown jewel, the Wellington Colliery, and the Victoria sales office. To signify the handover, Jim and Alex changed the company's name from Robert Dunsmuir & Sons to Robert Dunsmuir's Sons. They each owned 50 percent.

Joan and the daughters held a crisis management meeting. "What if Alex marries that woman?" they fretted. "That woman" was what Joan and the girls called Alex's mistress of two decades, Josephine Wallace.

While his father was alive, Alex had concealed from the family that he was living with Josephine, a beautiful buxom blonde who divorced her low-income bartender husband to be with super-rich Alex. Their affair started around 1881 when he was twenty-eight. Josephine was three years older and the mother of a boy, who lived with his father, and a girl, Edna, who went with Josephine. Alex paid for Edna's education at a private girls' boarding school and gifted Josephine a house in the San Francisco suburb of San Leandro, with the deed in her name. But Alex kept dodging Josephine's requests to get married, even after Robert died. He never took her to Victoria. The only member of the family who met Josephine was James, on a business trip to the San Francisco office, who informed his mother and sisters of the arrangement.

They were scandalized by Alex's behaviour, which was rather hypocritical considering Joan's pre-marital goings-on with Robert. But were they primarily upset on moral grounds or for financial reasons? Or maybe both? Alex and Josephine could be said to have a common-law marriage, but under then–California law, a common-law spouse wasn't entitled to anything if their significant other predeceased them. Moreover, in 1895 California abolished common-law marriage. As for legally recognized marriages, in 1890s' California, a wife was not automatically entitled to inherit her husband's entire estate, but was entitled to a portion of property acquired during the marriage — "community property" — and potentially some of his separate property.

Given a choice between Alex living "in sin" or his money wafting to Josephine if they married and he predeceased her, which seemed likely given his reckless drinking, Joan and the girls preferred the former.

Still, the daughters kept saying to their mother, "That woman could cause problems. Alex's drinking may very well kill him soon and she could inherit all he has. You have to protect yourself." Alex had had numerous episodes of alcohol-related delirium.

Their depiction of Alex as an unreliable drunken sot was reinforced by his inebriation on a stay at Craigdarroch in December 1896. The purpose of his visit was to get Joan to sign the transfer documents for the parts of the empire she'd promised him and James.

Totally hammered, Alex reeled into Joan's bedroom one night where she was propped up in bed by pillows. Weaving back and forth at the foot of her bed, he slurred loudly, "Mother, you must sign. You must. I won't leave this room until you do. You must." Joan shouted at him, "Get out of my room. You're mad. Get out of my room. Go back to bed." Their argument was so loud that it was heard throughout vast Craigdarroch. The servants listened avidly. They spread the story to friends working as servants in other households, who gossiped to their employers, and soon all of Victoria knew.

Joan insisted that James and Alex sign an agreement that if either of them died before her, his interest in Robert Dunsmuir's Sons would go to her. Both signed, perhaps thinking or hoping that the Grim Reaper would come for her first.

Three years later, on an afternoon in June 1899, Joan, now seventy-one, was relaxing in her second-floor suite at Craigdarroch when James stormed in. His intent was to get Joan to stop dithering about handing over ownership of the Wellington Colliery, the last piece of the Dunsmuir business empire still in her control, to him and Alex. Although most of its coal had been exhausted, the brothers believed the Wellington's fame would be helpful in attracting investors to new coal projects. Once again the servants at Craigdarroch eavesdropped and disseminated the details. According to them, James demanded, "Mother, stop stalling and give us the Wellington."

"If you want it so much, buy it," she retorted. "It'll cost you $500,000."

"That's outrageous," James angrily responded. "The mine is nearly played out."

Two months went by after this argument. Then, in August, Joan summoned James to Craigdarroch. According to the servants the quarrel picked up where it had left off earlier. "I hear that you're stripping the Wellington to devalue it. You're trying to rob me," she accused him.

"Don't listen to tittle-tattle," he snapped. He whipped out a bill of sale from his pocket and commanded, "Sign it." At this tense point, her doctor arrived on a house call to give her a regular checkup. Seeing that she was greatly agitated, alarmed that she could have a stroke or heart attack, the doctor ordered James to leave. James refused. "Mind your business or I'll throw you out the window," he shouted at the doctor.

Joan yelled at James, "Leave my house at once." Now both James and Alex were barred from the premises.

Joan never spoke to James or Alex again. She had her chief adviser, John Bryden, eldest daughter Elizabeth's husband, take over direct negotiations. He advised her to lower her price to $400,000, she acquiesced, and James and Alex accepted.

Ten years had now elapsed since Robert's death and will had ignited family warfare.

Alex finally agreed to Josephine Wallace's persistence that he marry her. Their wedding date was set for December 22, 1899. The day before, Alex wrote a will:

> I Alexander Dunsmuir of San Francisco California United States of America revoke all wills and testamentary disposal by me heretofore made and declare this to be my last will and testament. I give devise and bequeath all my property both real and personal wheresoever situate unto my brother James Dunsmuir of Victoria of British Columbia absolutely and I appoint the said James Dunsmuir sole executor of this my will. In testimony whereof I have herewith set my hand the twenty first day of December one thousand eight hundred and ninety-nine.

He kept the will secret from Josphine. Alex and Josephine were married for just forty days when he died on January 31, 1900, at age forty-seven. His death was attributed to "alcoholic dementia," today called "alcohol-related dementia," defined as "a severe form of alcohol-related brain damage caused by heavy alcohol consumption over a long period."

Like his father, Alex had left a simply worded will that caused many complications and much dissension within family ranks. It split the members further.

Per his will everything he had was to go to James, but the law in California, where Alex and Josephine resided, said a widow was to receive some of her husband's estate. James feared that she'd go after her late husband's interest in Robert Dunsmuir's Sons. Joan feared if that happened it would nullify the agreement James and Alex had signed on December 10, 1896, that should one of them predecease her, his half-interest was to go to her.

Knowing that Josephine was terminally ill with cancer, James, in his role as executor of Alex's estate, told Josephine he would pay her $25,000 a year in monthly installments but that she would have to waive her rights to any claims to Alex's estate. This was his way of keeping Alex's half-interest in Robert Dunsmuir's Sons for himself. Josephine was too sick to realize that James was tricking her and signed away her rights. She died June 22, 1901, eighteen months after Alex.

But James still had Joan to contend with, and she couldn't be manipulated. On October 30, 1901, four months after Josephine's death, Joan filed a lawsuit against James "for delivery of 4,998 shares in the firm of Robert Dunsmuir's Sons in pursuance of an agreement between the plaintiff, the defendant, and the late Alexander Dunsmuir." In 1901 James was in his second year as premier of British Columbia. "PREMIER OF BRITISH COLUMBIA SUED BY HIS MOTHER," newspaper headlines blazed.

Concurrently, it turned out that he hadn't got rid of the Josephine situation. All of a sudden, a new character entered the fray — Josephine's heir, her now adult daughter, Edna Wallace Hopper, a popular Broadway actress-comic opera singer.

Edna had been a young girl when her mom and Alex began their affair. At the age of fifteen, she dropped out of school and went to New York,

America's live theatre capital, and, desiring to become a stage actress, made the rounds of auditions. Pretty and vivacious, she was soon hired. Over the years she became a featured player with billing just below the top star. In 1900 Edna played the important role of Lady Holyrood, described as "a lady of title but little else," in the smash hit comedy *Floradora*.

Edna was unabashedly, flagrantly uninhibited in an era in which the rules were that women be inhibited. She had numerous affairs with wealthy men. She loved publicity, good or bad — it didn't matter to her as long as she got her name in the papers and attracted crowds to her shows.

As Josephine's sole beneficiary, Edna inherited the mansion Alex had gifted Josephine. But she wanted more. She began calling herself Alex's stepdaughter. She asked her lover at the time, a wealthy Wall Street financier, to make it possible for her to sue James. He got her a big-name lawyer and promised to pay the lawyer's fees. Edna liked to do things in a big way. She launched not one but two lawsuits against James in early 1902, one in San Francisco, the other in Victoria, to get a chunk of Alex's estate.

Then, something astonishing happened. Joan, up until now "do-it-herself-Joan" in conflicts with James, decided to support Edna's action in British Columbia's Supreme Court to "set aside," or void, Alex's will. Who approached who is unknown, but it's an amazing twist to the story in that Joan had earlier said, "I'd rather see Alex in his grave than married to that woman [Josephine]."

But, as the saying goes, "My enemy's enemy is my friend." When Edna travelled to Victoria, she stayed at the Driard Hotel, Victoria's then premier hotel, whose mortgages were held by Joan. Did Edna stay there on her own initiative because it was the premier hotel or did Joan arrange it? The answer is unknown, but it's fun to speculate about whether the two women got together at the Driard or Craigdarroch to plot strategy over tea and scones.

The trial took place in 1903. Joan didn't testify; instead, she had her daughters take the stand to bolster Edna's case. The gist of it was that Alexander was a drunk and suffering from "cerebral meningitis" (which alcoholism can cause) when he signed the will giving James his estate. "The trial established the fact that Alexander Dunsmuir was a godsend to the liquor industry of California," said *The Vancouver Daily World*. "But it also showed extensive though his capacity was for cocktails and such like 'insidious' drinks, yet it did not interfere with his capacity for business, as the judge put it."

On February 6, 1904, BC Supreme Court Justice Montague Tyrwhitt-Drake ruled in James's favour. Edna and Joan continued their fight all the way up to the Judicial Committee of the Privy Council in London, England, which had the authority to overrule the Supreme Court of Canada up to 1949. It, too, ruled in James's favour. The California court also ruled in his favour. Alex's will would remain in effect.

Not only did Edna lose, but by that time she was cash-strapped after her wealthy sugar daddy had dumped her and taken up with another woman. Adding to her financial burden, as executor of Josephine's estate, it was her legal obligation to pay all valid debts, claims, and taxes on the estate, and Josephine had died owing debts of $38,000. To afford to pay, Edna sold the San Leandro mansion she'd inherited from Josephine.

Edna and Joan's alliance of convenience ended. But Edna wasn't in financial difficulty for long. Her career was boosted by the publicity her case had generated. She started a cosmetics line and in 1908 married Albert Oldfield Brown, an actor who later became president of The Lambs Club, a prominent social club in New York City for actors, songwriters, and others involved in the theatre.

As for James, he'd won the power struggle with Joan and was appointed lieutenant governor of British Columbia in 1906, which he celebrated by commissioning the construction in Victoria of a castle of his own, Hatley, a rival to Joan's Craigdarroch castle. "Money doesn't matter, just build what I want," James said, sounding a lot like his father, who'd replied when someone said Craigdarroch would cost a fortune, "Then it's a good thing I have a fortune."

Hatley Castle's grounds were 650 acres compared to Craigdarroch's twenty-eight. It had forty rooms, one more than Craigdarroch. The wall surrounding the estate cost over $75,000; the conservatory, costing a like amount, was filled with white orchids imported from India, and a large banana tree stood in the centre under the dome. The rooms of the house were filled with flowers from the conservatory throughout the year. Six miles of road interlaced the estate, and a hundred men were employed in the gardens. The estate had a refrigeration plant; cow barns; a slaughterhouse and a smoke house; three silos, each with a hundred-ton capacity; and a reserve water tank.

James was as ruthless an employer as Robert had been. To prevent unionization he used threats, spies, blacklists, and scab labour, as well as exerting his influence to have the provincial government call in the militia. He was uncaring about unsafe mine conditions and explosions that killed workers.

Joan, meanwhile, continued to fight James for Alex's half of Robert Dunsmuir's Sons, filing a new lawsuit on September 18, 1908, at age eighty. The case never went to court as she died two weeks later, on October 2, 1908.

Her will was the third Dunsmuir will that caused an uproar. Her five surviving daughters were her heirs. James, of course, was excluded. At issue was how much her taxable estate was worth. The lower its value, the lower succession duties would be for the daughters to pay. The issue was so complicated that the probate court was bewildered and the British Columbia Supreme Court stepped in to sort it out. The daughters said its value was $381,700; the tax department said $854,000; and finally in April 1909, six months after Joan's death, the Supreme Court declared $794,000.

The daughters frittered away what they got.

In 1910, James, then nearing sixty, sold off the Dunsmuir collieries, coal rights in the Esquimalt and Nanaimo Railway Belt, and everything else in the Robert Dunsmuir business empire and retired. The buyers were William Mackenzie and Donald Mann, promoters of the Canadian Northern Railway, a transcontinental rival to the Canadian Pacific Railway. They paid $11 million ($285.5 million today). This was considerably less than the $15 million value placed on founder Robert Dunsmuir's financial worth when he died twenty-five years earlier.

When James died ten years later, his estate was valued at $3,332,000 ($86.5 million today), $8 million less than the money he'd received for the Dunsmuir business. He'd spent considerable sums on the upkeep of Hatley Castle, plus the acquisition of an enormous yacht custom built for him in Scotland. To give an idea of its size, the dining room sat two dozen people. He also lost money on bad investments.

In successive generations, the once powerful feuding family faded from the spotlight. None of Robert Dunsmuir's descendants would recoup his fame or fortune. With any luck, however, perhaps they were able to restore peace within the family.

8

RACIST?

What is the responsibility of a trustee when a will may be against the public good? This chapter provides examples, and, intriguingly, the decisions vary.

In one example, a Black man in Ontario cut one of his daughters out of his will because she'd had an affair with a white man and a son by him, but included his other daughter, who was married to a Black man and had two sons by him.

In another example, a white man cut out non-whites, non-heterosexuals, people who weren't single, feminists, and intercollegiate sports participants from a scholarship that was to be set up following his death. It stipulated that no more than 25 percent of the scholarship funds could be allocated annually to female students.

In both instances trustees had been appointed by the deceased to administer their wills.

Was their duty to unquestioningly carry out the will's instructions, or was their duty to the public not to? Were the wills testamentary freedom or racist? If declared testamentary freedom, the money would go to the beneficiaries specified in the wills. If declared racist, the wills would be declared void and the court would rule where the money should go.

The opposing sides went to court over both wills, and in both instances the restrictions made in an Ontario public trust set up ninety years earlier, the Leonard trust, were discussed at length as pertinent.

The Ninety-Year-Old Leonard Trust

The earlier public trust discussed in both cases involved Reuben Wells Leonard (1860–1930), an Ontario businessman who'd made a fortune in mining in northern Ontario and in 1923 established a charitable trust in his name, The Leonard Foundation, to provide educational scholarships. But the trust wasn't available to much of the nation because of Leonard's bigoted views. The trust stipulated that the scholarships were available only to white, Protestant, British subjects, and that no more than 25 percent of the scholarship funds could be allocated annually to female students. "The trust reflected Leonard's deeply held ideologies," the *Dictionary of Canadian Biography* entry on him says. "He believed in the superiority of the white race, and in the importance of Christianity and the British empire in ensuring the progress of civilization." Leonard's view was that "there are vast and ineradicable differences among races."

Leonard had carefully cultivated an image of himself as a successful businessman who viewed his great wealth as a public trust. He gave money generously to educational institutions, the Anglican Church, and hospitals and served on the boards of a number of Canadian universities. He was hailed by many as an exemplary philanthropist.

But one of the reasons he was ultra-rich was that he severely underpaid his workers. The price of Canadian minerals rose substantially following the end of the First World War, which meant that mine owners like Leonard were piling up profits. They wouldn't have been rolling in dough without the hard work of their employees, but when the employees sought a wage hike, the mine owners refused. They also snuffed out the workers' attempts to unionize. The workers went on strike; Leonard and the other owners waited them out, and the workers were as badly off as ever. This makes Leonard's guise of kindly benefactor even in his lifetime selective at best.

When Leonard announced his 1923 trust fund, it was praised as yet another example of "generous philanthropy by Leonard." It wasn't until the

1960s when the civil rights and women's rights movements gathered steam that Leonard's exclusionary criteria came under scrutiny, and still decades later that legal action was taken.

In 1986 a complaint filed against the foundation under the Ontario Human Rights Code prompted litigation by the Ontario Human Rights Commission against the trust's administrator, Canada Trust. As trustee, Canada Trust's obligation was to carry out the instructions of the person who had created the trust, to be neutral, and to let a court decide if a variation was necessary in view of changing public attitudes.

In 1990 the Ontario Court of Appeal held that the terms relating to race, religion, nationality, and gender in the Leonard trust were contrary to public policy. Justice Sydney Lewis Robins said, "The trust was valid and not contrary to public policy when created in 1923. However, with changing social attitudes, public policy also has changed. As a result, the continuation of the trust as originally contemplated is no longer in the public interest. It is impracticable to carry it on in the manner originally intended by the settlor." The court came up with a nifty solution: It excised the offensive terms, then said the money could still be used on the proviso that it help all students. This was done and the foundation still exists.

Black-Only Will

Eric Spence was born in Jamaica in 1942. He moved to England circa the early 1960s. He had what was described by the court as "a relationship" with a woman whose name was never disclosed in documents. They had a daughter, Verolin, in 1963 and another, Donna, in 1964. Eric and the woman parted ways not long after, and in 1979 he immigrated to the Toronto area. There he married a woman named Norma, a nurse at Branson Hospital in Toronto. The couple had no children of their own.

After their parents broke up, Verolin lived with her father and Donna with her mother. The two sisters didn't communicate with each other after the separation. Eric never expressed an interest in visiting Donna, nor did she ever visit him while he was in England or later in Canada.

Verolin said that from the time of their parents' separation, Donna had "little or no contact" with Eric. "She certainly never lived with him nor did my father express any intention to contact Donna. In fact, her name never came up in any of our conversations. Donna's sons Kairo and Kailen never met him nor had any contact with him. As far as I know, my father never provided any financial support to Donna, Kairo, or Kailen."

In marked contrast, Eric paid for all of Verolin's eight years of university education and her living expenses during that time. She got a Bachelor of Arts degree in history at York University in Toronto, then attended the University of London (England) Institute of Education, where she got a post-graduate certificate in education, business studies, and economics and a Master of Arts degree in education in multiculturalism. She then went to the New York School of Law at Queen's College, part of the City University of New York, from which she graduated with a law degree.

She said, "My father placed a great deal of emphasis on education. He was very pleased and proud of my educational accomplishments. He provided me with support and tuition for my eight years of post-secondary education.

"We had an excellent relationship. He told me he'd made a will which provided that I would inherit the home and gave me a set of keys allowing me unlimited and continued use of it."

Their relationship disintegrated in September 2002 when she told him that she was pregnant by a white man. Verolin gave birth to a boy on April 26, 2003. Eric refused to have anything to do with her or his grandson and disinherited them from his will written in 2010, saying,

> I specifically bequeath nothing to my daughter [Verolin], as she has had no communication with me for several years and has shown no interest in me as her father.

After a money bequest to a cousin, leaving his jewellery to Donna's sons and his personal possessions and household items to his wife, Norma, or if she predeceased him to Donna, he willed the residue to be divided in equal shares among Donna and her sons. Norma died in 2011, the year after he wrote his will.

Imogene Parchment, a long-time friend and co-worker of Norma's at Branson Hospital, said Norma, when dying, had asked her to take care of Eric, who was in poor health. Imogene found Eric to be abrasive. "I visited him several times every week to attend to his needs. He was a difficult person. He had an explosive temper and was demanding. He had virtually no friends and mistreated his agency caregivers to the point where the agency stopped sending them."

Eric suffered a stroke on Christmas Day, 2012. While he was in hospital, no one visited him other than Imogene Parchment. He died a month later, on January 25, 2013. The only people who attended his funeral were friends of Norma's.

His estate was valued at $398,875, and the trustee named in his will was BMO Trust Company, a division of the Bank of Montreal.

In October 2014, Verolin applied to Ontario's Superior Court for Eric's will to be voided, maintaining that it was "racially motivated and therefore contrary to public policy." A court can void a will if it deems it's against public policy, which racism is in Canada. Verolin said: "When he found out that the father of my child was white, my father told me that he was ashamed of me. From that point onwards, my father restricted his communications with me. He wouldn't return my phone calls. He made it very clear to me that he would not allow a 'white man's child' in his house. The reason my father severed the relationship with me is because I gave birth to a child fathered by a white man."

Imogene Parchment said she'd known Verolin as well as Eric for many years and was well aware of the situation. "When he found out that the father of Verolin's son wasn't black he told me that he had no further use for Verolin and, quote, 'her bastard white son.' He told me on several occasions that he disinherited Verolin and her son because the father of her son was white. He changed his will on May 12, 2010, because he wanted to exclude Verolin and include Donna and her two sons since the father of Donna's sons was black."

According to Imogene, a short time after Eric signed this will, he quarrelled with Donna. "He told me that he had had a fight with his daughter Donna on the telephone and that he would never call her again nor did he want anything to do with her."

She said she tried to intervene: "About two weeks before his death I spoke to him about the possibility of reconciling with his two daughters. He went into a rage, banging his fists on the table and told me that he had changed his will, removing both his daughters and their children as beneficiaries." However, a new will disinheriting Donna was never discovered.

According to Imogene, Eric and Donna were never close. "She never visited him, and he never visited her. Donna told me by phone after he died that she'd never been to Canada. She didn't come to his funeral. She never expressed that she was sorry that she wouldn't be attending her father's funeral." Imogene concluded: "It's clear to me that the reason he excluded Verolin from his will and included Donna and her sons was because Verolin had a child with a man who wasn't black and he wanted to discriminate against her."

The legal term for what Verolin and Imogene said is "extrinsic (from without) evidence" — opinions about the context and intent apart from what's said in a document, in this instance a will. A court may or may not give extrinsic evidence weight.

During the court proceedings, the Reuben Wells Leonard charitable trust mentioned earlier in this chapter was brought up. As the Leonard case involved a public trust, it readily qualified for public examination of whether it was unacceptable and against public policy / the public good. Private trusts, however, aren't as easy to challenge on these grounds. In its capacity as trustee, BMO Trust's duty in principle was to do what it had been entrusted to do, to see to it that Eric Spence's wishes regarding his estate were carried out. The trustee supported Spence, saying, "The 'disinheritance clause' of the will is unambiguous, unequivocal, and unconditional and contains none of the unsavoury or patently discriminatory provisions of the type at issue in *Canada Trust.* Additionally, Eric's bequest of the residue of his estate is of a private, rather than a public, nature."

If the Ontario Superior Court ruled that Eric's will was against public policy, he would be deemed to have died "intestate" — without a will under the terms of Ontario's 1990 Succession Law Reform Act. When this happens a judge rules on how the estate should be distributed. Usually, it's split between next of kin.

On January 27, 2015, Ontario Superior Court Justice Cory A. Gilmore, "the application judge," gave her decision. Her opening words probably caused Verolin to fret that she was going to lose: "On its face clause 5(h) doesn't offend public policy." The justice, however, was by no means finished. As she spoke on, Verolin must have started to relax. The justice continued:

> Were it not for the unchallenged evidence of Ms. Parchment and Verolin, the court would have no alternative but to go no further than the wording in the will. But given the uncontradicted and clear extrinsic evidence, Eric's reason for disinheriting Verolin was based on a clearly stated racist principle and the provisions of the will favouring Donna and her sons to the exclusion of Verolin offended not only human sensibilities but also public policy.

That said, Justice Gilmore "set aside" (voided) the will "in its entirety" on the basis that it "violated public policy against discrimination on racial grounds." She declared Eric to have died intestate and said the estate should be divided equally between Verolin and Donna. The effect was to wholly disinherit Donna's sons, named beneficiaries under Eric's will.

BMO Trust vaulted upward to the Ontario Court of Appeal asking it to overturn the application judge's decision. Verolin took part in the hearing, but Donna and her sons didn't, just as they hadn't in the application hearing.

BMO Trust maintained that the application judge

- "erred by placing weight on the extrinsic evidence because it is contradictory and inconsistent";
- "unjustifiably interfered with Eric's testamentary freedom to distribute his property as he chooses"; and
- "did not have jurisdiction to set aside the entire Will."

The Court of Appeal said the bank was right and overturned the lower court's decision. When a lower and higher court reach diametrically opposite conclusions, it's usually due to differences in interpretation of existing laws and legal precedents and the "facts" in the case. If a person disagrees with a court, they can go to a higher one, bearing in mind that their legal bills will balloon and they could very well lose again.

White-Only Will

Victor Hugh Priebe (1931–2015) was a radiologist at Hôtel-Dieu Grace Hospital in Windsor, Ontario. He never married nor had children. His closest relative, sister Helen, had predeceased him. He wrote his will on July 2, 1994, shortly before he retired. He lived twenty-one more years and never changed it, indicative that the prejudiced thinking he expressed in it was unyielding.

Priebe wrote in paragraph 3(d)(ii)(E) of his will:

> To provide funds, from time to time and in the discretion of my Trustee for awards or bursaries to Caucasian (white), male, single, heterosexual students in scientific studies, including medicine, genetics, biology, chemistry, physics, and those going into medical pharmacology research.
>
> It is my wish that academic achievement be taken into consideration but not necessarily the highest marks, but a minimum cumulative average of at least 10.0 (B+) and an honest desire to work and achieve. Extracurricular activities (i.e. non-academic) of the applicant shall not be taken into consideration in qualifying a student for purpose of these awards or bursaries.
>
> In addition, students with the necessary academic qualifications who have demonstrated that they are not afraid of hard manual work in their selection of summer employment shall be given special consideration in the selection process. If no paid employment is available, then a full-time voluntary manual labour job may be considered as a substitute.
>
> These awards shall be directed to students who are going to attend the University of Western Ontario or those for whom it may be a hardship to go to the University

> of Western Ontario then they can be awarded to these particular students who wish to attend the University of Windsor. No awards to be given to anyone who plays intercollegiate sports.
>
> Further, to similarly provide funds for an award to be known as the Ellen O'Donnel Priebe Memorial Award [named after his mother] under the same terms as the awards above, except this award is to go to a hard-working, single, Caucasian white girl who is not a feminist or lesbian, with special consideration, if she is an immigrant, but not necessarily a recent one. This award is for someone going into a field of scientific study (not medicine) on the terms outlined above for the male applicants.

As Priebe hadn't selected trustees, the Ontario Superior Court appointed Royal Trust, a Canadian trust fund company. It thought Priebe's restrictions were repugnant. Whereas decades earlier another trust fund company, Canada Trust, had abided by Reuben Wells Leonard's biases in his trust until it was challenged in court by the Ontario Human Rights Commission, Royal Trust immediately leaped into action. Times had changed: It was now politically incorrect to exclude and marginalize particular groups. Moreover, it was illegal under the Canadian Charter of Rights and Freedoms, which came into effect in 1982, twelve years before Priebe died. Section 15, "Equality of Rights," says, "Every individual is equal before and under the law and has the right to the equal protection and equal benefit of the law without discrimination and, in particular, without discrimination based on race, national or ethnic origin, colour, religion, sex, age or mental or physical disability."

Royal Trust went to the Ontario Superior Court for guidance in what was called *Royal Trust Corporation of Canada v. The University of Western Ontario et al.* The hearing was presided over by Ontario Superior Court Justice A. (Alyssa) K. Mitchell on February 16, 2016. It wasn't adversarial against the University of Western Ontario and the University of Windsor — they were cited because Priebe had put them in charge of dispersing the educational bursaries. He hadn't asked them if they were willing; they had had nothing to do with his decision and had been dragged in. The universities didn't utter a peep of protest against being named and by their silence made clear that they supported what Royal Trust was doing. Like Royal Trust, the two universities didn't want to be perceived as endorsing Priebe's views.

Royal Trust asked for the Ontario Superior Court to give its "opinion, advice, and direction" on five points:

> (a) Does the will provide the trustee with a discretion to choose whether or not to disperse funds for the purpose of para. 3(d)(ii)(E) of the will?
>
> (b) Are any of the provisions in para. 3(d)(ii)(E) of the will void or illegal or not capable of being lawfully administered by the trustee because they are contrary to public policy, discriminatory on the basis of race, creed, citizenship, ancestry, place of origin, colour, ethnic origin, sexual orientation or otherwise and/or uncertain?
>
> (c) If so, who is entitled to the trust funds under the will?
>
> (d) Is there a general charitable intention expressed in the will sufficient to permit the court to exercise its inherent jurisdiction in the matter of charitable trusts and direct that the trust be administered cy-pres?
>
> (e) If the court exercises its inherent jurisdiction to direct that the trust be administered cy-pres, how should the trustee administer the trusts?

The term "cy-pres" is derived from an old French phrase, *cy près comme possible,* which in English translates to "as close as possible." It comes into play when the expressed purpose in a will or trust or other documents is impossible and/or impracticable to fulfill. The entire document isn't voided, only the objectionable parts, thereby "saving" the good parts to benefit all, not the chosen few selected by the author of the document.

Justice Mitchell declared paragraph 3(d)(ii)(E) "void as being contrary to public policy by virtue of it being discriminatory on the basis of race, gender and sexual orientation." But she didn't implement cy-pres. She didn't need to because Priebe had in effect done this in section G of his will:

> In the event that one or more of the foregoing provisions shall be declared to be of a non-charitable nature, or, if the qualifications set forth for receipt of an award referred to above are adjudged by a court of competent jurisdiction to be void for public policy, then the provision for such gift shall be deleted without prejudice to the remaining provisions of this paragraph 3(d)(ii).

Which raises the question: If he realized that clause 3(d)(ii)(E) could cause his will to be voided as against public policy, why did he include it?

9

THE NEO-NAZI WILL

Harry Robert McCorkill, a New Brunswick resident at the time of his death in April 2004 at age sixty-seven, willed his entire estate ($250,000 in antiquity coins) to an American-based neo-Nazi organization, the National Alliance, of which he was a member. Whether this should happen went to the Supreme Court of Canada, a landmark case. The pivotal issue was "freedom of expression" — limits per Canada's Charter of Rights and Freedoms, or no caveats per the United States' Constitution.

McCorkill had been a shadowy, secretive, nomadic person. He'd never married and had no children. He'd been out of touch for many years with his sister and brother, who wanted nothing to do with him because of his Nazi sympathies. Following his death, it took two weeks for authorities to determine if he had any next of kin. During that time McCorkill's body was kept in storage. When his next of kin were finally found, his sister and brother had no interest in paying for his burial.

Jennifer Pritchett, a reporter with the Saint John, New Brunswick, *Telegraph-Journal*, wrote that McCorkill had lived in a townhouse in Millidgeville, a suburb on the northern edge of Saint John, for about a year before his death and according to neighbours "had kept to himself." Before that, he had been a resident of both Saskatchewan and Ontario.

Pritchett also unearthed the following story of what happened after McCorkill's death in her newspaper article:

> The National Alliance paid for his funeral and hired Malcolm Ross and William Ross of Moncton to transport, store and take inventory of his assets. Malcolm Ross was the focus of a 1996 Supreme Court ruling that found that the former Moncton-area teacher whose off-duty writings claimed Christians were under attack by an international Jewish conspiracy, "had poisoned the educational environment." The ruling upheld a human rights board of inquiry that ordered Ross into a non-teaching job.

The neo-Nazi National Alliance (NA) was an American organization established in 1974 by William Luther Pierce, a scientist born in Atlanta, Georgia, in 1933. Pierce, who came from a long line of Confederates, believed that Black persons were "naturally subordinate" to white persons, whom he called the "superior race." He had been involved with a number of Nazi organizations before founding the NA.

In 1985 he divorced his wife, declaring it "necessary in order for me to have the peace of mind I need to do most effectively what I must do with my life," and abandoned his son. He bought 346 acres in a remote area of West Virginia and built a compound "where a new kind of family — men and women of like mind — could live off the land and be free of outside influences." He moved into a rambling trailer home where he lived with a series of what he called "wives."

He was an individual with what are defined as the characteristics of a cult leader — "a charismatic, self-appointed leader, who tightly controls members, requiring unwavering devotion to beliefs and practices outside the norms of society." His was a cult of bigotry and hate.

Pierce made $1 million from a hate propaganda business empire he built of white supremacist, anti-Semitic writings, records, and a radio program. In the 1990s the Federal Bureau of Investigation labelled the NA the largest and most influential white nationalist group in the United States. It had adherents in other countries too, including Harry Robert McCorkill in Canada, who was said to have stayed at Pierce's compound.

The NA was as explicitly genocidal against Jews as Hitler, who Pierce idolized, had been. Pierce's goal was to make the United States into a Nazi-like country in which the NA, with him as führer, would rule the nation.

He authored a "white power" novel, *The Turner Diaries*, which advocated an uprising of white supremacists to eradicate non-whites, Jews, and other minorities in the United States and establish an all-white homeland. Photocopies of pages were found in the car driven by Timothy McVeigh the day he bombed the Oklahoma City federal building in 1995, killing 168 people, including nineteen children.

According to the Southern Poverty Law Centre (SPLC), NA members "were connected to at least 14 violent crimes between 1984 and 2005, including bank robberies, shootouts with police and, in Orlando, Florida, a plan to bomb the main approach to Disney World." Estimates of the NA's membership circa 2002, when McCorkill had been a member for four years, ranged from 1,400 to 2,500.

McCorkill's will, dated April 19, 2000, named William Luther Pierce of Post Office Box 70, Hillsboro, West Virginia, as his sole executor and trustee and Fred Gene Streed of the same address as his alternate. (The NA's headquarters weren't in Hillsboro but in the vicinity.) In the will, McCorkill transferred all of his property to his trustee "in trust to pay all my debts and taxes and to pay or transfer the residue of my estate to the NATIONAL ALLIANCE, a Virginia corporation, with principal offices at Post Office Box 70, Hillsboro, West Virginia 24946, United States of America," the same address he used for both his executor, also Pierce, and alternate executor, Streed.

Pierce died in July 2002 at age sixty-eight of kidney failure and cancer, which made Streed the will's executor and trustee of McCorkill's estate when McCorkill died in 2004. It took six years for Streed to apply to New Brunswick's court of probate for letters of probate. Letters of probate provide official recognition of the authority of the executor over the testator's estate. Why had Streed waited six years? The delay likely was due to the National Alliance spinning into disarray after Pierce's death.

The organization was racked by infighting, power struggles, mishandling of money, dwindling income, and damaging exposés by the SPLC including its release of a videotape of Pierce's last speech in which he badmouthed other hate groups as "freaks and weaklings" and "human defectives." The SPLC also revealed that Erich Gliebe, a one-time boxer who was Pierce's successor, patronized strip clubs and had hired strippers to pose as "Aryan beauties" in an NA calendar. The scandals and turmoil resulted in the NA's membership plummeting by more than 50 percent within one year after Pierce's death. By 2007, the NA was down to about a hundred members. The SPLC says, "By 2009 the Alliance, once the ideological and criminal powerhouse of the American radical right, had become almost irrelevant."

The havoc within the NA was at full blast while McCorkill was still alive, but he didn't change his will. No doubt the tatters of the organization would have welcomed the infusion of his quarter of a million dollars.

Usually, letters of probate are issued in a matter of weeks, although it sometimes takes a month or even a year, but three years passed before Streed received his on May 6, 2013. Why the long wait? It's possible the court of probate was very reluctant to issue them considering the contents of the will.

The issuance of the letters spurred a number of people into action, beginning with McCorkill's sister, Isabelle Rose McCorkill, who launched a legal battle against the will. She said, "It isn't about the money but rather a reflection of my moral duty to intervene in an offensive and illegal bequest."

Isabelle retained Moncton, New Brunswick, lawyer Marc-Antoine Chiasson, who had previously gained national attention as principal counsel to the Commission of Inquiry into Pathology Services at the Miramichi, New Brunswick, Regional Health Authority, which investigated why there had been misdiagnoses of breast and prostate cancer tests, who was responsible, and how to prevent anything like it in the future.

On July 18, 2013, Chiasson filed an application in Isabelle's name to New Brunswick's Court of Queen's Bench — the province's highest trial court, which has jurisdiction over probate — against the executor of the estate, Streed, "to prevent the disposition of her brother's estate to the National Alliance." Chiasson said in explanation, "The National Alliance is a neo-Nazi organization and a gift to such a group is against public policy."

The court reacted speedily, issuing an injunction on July 22, just four days later, prohibiting Streed from transferring any portion of McCorkill's estate to the United States. On July 31 the order was extended until the application was heard in court.

At this point a number of other parties decided to get involved on both sides. Isabelle got support from the province (represented by the office of New Brunswick's attorney general), the Centre for Israel and Jewish Affairs, and the League for Human Rights of B'nai Brith Canada. All three were given leave on August 19 to "intervene." "Given leave to intervene" is legalese for allowing third parties to make arguments in a case. The Southern Poverty Law Center sent copies of its investigations into the National Alliance for submission by Chiasson.

The province took part because the Human Rights Act of New Brunswick includes religion, race, colour, and ancestry on its list of protections against "discrimination and implicitly harassment." The interveners supporting Isabelle maintained that the National Alliance's profile had declined with the death of its founder, Pierce, and that "the bequest would provide funds to the organization to resurrect itself and its mandate to deny the Holocaust, and promote racial cleansing and genocide."

On August 29, Isabelle via Chiasson submitted an amended application, asking for the court to issue an order voiding McCorkill's bequest to the National Alliance. The application specified an opinion as to why the will was contrary to public policy:

> (i) The National Alliance is a long-standing neo-Nazi group in the United States that has also been active in Canada. Through its hate propaganda, the National Alliance promotes a political program parallel to that of the original World War II-era National Socialist Party of Germany (the Nazis) including genocide, ethnic cleansing, and the use of hate motivated violence and terror to achieve its aims.
> (ii) The National Alliance has a long history of inspiring and carrying out hate motivated violence and terror

> through its members and supporters in order to achieve its stated political aims;
> (iii) The Criminal Code of Canada specifically prohibits hate propaganda in Canada and makes criminal offences of advocating genocide and publicly inciting hatred;
> (iv) Canada has been a signatory and party to the International Convention on the Elimination of All Forms of Racial Discrimination since 1970. It says: "Parties to the Convention shall condemn all hate propaganda and declare as offences hate propaganda, membership in racial supremacist groups and the provision of any assistance to racist activities, including the financing thereof";
> (v) Canada has also signed on, and committed to, other international declarations and covenants which specifically protect individuals against any discrimination, advocacy of national, racial, or religious hatred and incitement to discrimination and violence.

Streed was represented by Moncton lawyer John D. Hughes. In 1993, Hughes had been one of the lawyers for Malcolm Ross, the Moncton man whom the National Alliance hired to "preserve" McCorkill's assets after his death, in Ross's claim of defamation lawsuit against Saint John, New Brunswick, *Telegraph-Journal* cartoonist Josh Beutel. Beutel's cartoon had depicted Ross as being like Hitler's propaganda minister Joseph Goebbels. After the province's lower trial court, the Court of Queen's Bench, ruled in Ross's favour, ordering that Beutel pay $7,500 in compensation, Beutel went to the New Brunswick Court of Appeal, which dismissed the fine and awarded Beutel court costs.

On September 3, 2013, the Canadian Association for Free Expression (CAFE), a far-right group founded in 1981, succeeded in getting accepted as an intervenor too. (Hate groups tend to have bland, misleading names.) The association took exception to several passages in affidavits from Mark Potok of the Southern Poverty Law Center and Anita Bromberg, national director of legal affairs at B'nai Brith Canada, describing them as "not fact, but opinion and argumentative," and asked that they be declared inadmissible.

CAFE cited section 2, "Fundamental Freedoms," clause 2(b) of Canada's Charter of Rights and Freedoms: "freedom of thought, belief, opinion, and expression, including freedom of the press and other media of communication." It said the will "should stand as representing Mr. McCorkill's wishes which were paramount and should not be subject to court intervention simply because the intended beneficiary espouses a message that is unpopular or even contrary to Canada's Criminal Code and Charter of Rights and Freedoms."

CAFE also argued that it "wasn't up to a judge to determine the worthiness of a beneficiary" and to do so "would open a Pandora's box," illustrating its point by querying whether a bequest "to the Hell's Angels or a drug dealer or even to Greenpeace could be subject to attack."

It referred to the Saskatchewan Court of Queen's Bench and then the higher Saskatchewan Court of Appeal case of *Bolianatz Estate v. Simon* (discussed in Chapter 2), which gave the go-ahead for a bequest in a will to proceed even though the recipient had stolen from the will's author. "This decision," CAFE argued, "is relevant to McCorkill's will because it said the testator's perception of the beneficiary was what mattered and that it should not be interfered with."

The New Brunswick Court of Queen's Bench hearing regarding Harry McCorkill's will took place from January 27 to 28, 2014, before Justice William T. Grant. Neither Isabella Rose McCorkill nor Fred Streed attended; they didn't have to, and their lawyers appeared on their behalf.

Justice Grant released his decision on June 5, 2014. Ten years had gone by since Harry McCorkill's death. Grant emphasized the difference between Canada and the United States in the interpretation of "free speech." He thought America allowed too much latitude.

Grant began:

> Much of the content of the affidavits filed by the respondent [Streed] focused on discrediting the SPLC's evidence as being deliberately misleading, containing half

truths and implying guilt by association. However, even if I accept every allegation these deponents make against the SPLC, that does not change the writings of the NA from William Luther Pierce 20 years ago to Erich Gliebe and others today, along with their foundational documents, Mr. Pierce's writings, their website, their other publications, and the transcripts of Mr. Gliebe's radio broadcasts. All of these publications can only be described as racist, white supremacist and hate-inspired. They are disgusting, repugnant and revolting.

While they may be protected by the first amendment under the US Constitution, there is a difference between that Constitution and the Canadian Charter of Rights and Freedoms which protects freedom of speech under Section 2(b) but also provides under Section 1 thereof:

The Canadian Charter of Rights and Freedoms guarantees the rights and freedoms set out in it subject only to such reasonable limits prescribed by law as can be demonstrably justified in a free and democratic society.

Section 319 of the Criminal Code of Canada makes the public incitement of hatred a criminal offence. Section 319(2) states:

> (2) Every one who, by communicating statements, other than in private conversation, willfully promotes hatred against any identifiable group is guilty of
> (a) an indictable offence and is liable to imprisonment for a term not exceeding two years; or
> (b) an offence punishable on summary conviction.

This court takes judicial notice of the fact that in this age of the internet national boundaries are meaningless for purposes of spreading hate propaganda such as that

> disseminated by the NA. In that regard I also accept and rely on the evidence of Anita Bromberg [B'nai Brith] that white supremacist groups in Canada share ties with American groups and interact with them on web forums.

Grant then addressed whether the will should be "voided" per Isabella's application that it was a violation of public policy in Canada. He said he agreed that the will was in violation:

> Public policy embodies the "interests of society" as expressed in the morals of the time, the common law and legislation. In my view engaging in activity which is prohibited by Parliament through the enactment of the Criminal Code of Canada falls squarely within the rubric of a public policy violation. In addition, as the applicant has pointed out, the NA's various communications and activities contravene the values set out in the Charter of Rights, provincial human rights legislation as well as the International Conventions which Canada has signed, all of which promote equality and the dignity of the person while prohibiting discrimination based on various grounds, including race and ethnic origin.
>
> The Court of Appeal has made the point on more than one occasion that trial judges must not "check their common sense at the court room door." Allowing this bequest to stand because it doesn't repeat those stated purposes but bestows the bequest on the organization whose very existence is dedicated to achieving them would be doing just that in my view.

He voided the will, leaving McCorkill to have died without a will, or intestate, and for the court to determine where the money should go. Grant said McCorkill's estate should be divided among Harry Robert McCorkill's next of kin.

This wasn't the end of the story about Harry Robert McCorkill's neo-Nazi will.

Nine months later, on March 3, 2015, Streed, with the Canadian Association for Free Expression as intervener on his behalf, asked the New Brunswick Court of Appeal to overrule Grant. The Court rejected the appeal on July 30, 2015, in one paragraph, again stating that the National Alliance's activities and messaging were "illegal and contrary to the public policy of Canada and New Brunswick."

In a last-ditch attempt, Streed, with the support of the Canadian Association for Free Expression, appealed to the Supreme Court of Canada, which dismissed his application.

Mark Potok, editor-in-chief of the SPLC journal *Intelligence Report*, praised the Canadian system when writing about McCorkill's will in an article titled "From Canada, With Love":

> The case against the bequest could never have been made under American law, which has unusually strong free speech and association protections. But Canadian law has a much fuller concept of the public good, and its foundational Canadian Charter of Rights and Freedoms allows speech and other "reasonable limits prescribed by law as can be demonstrably justified in a free and democratic society." Canadian law also makes public "incitement of hatred" — "willfully promoting hatred against any identifiable group" — a criminal offense.

Although Canadian courts rarely interfere with a person's freedom to choose to whom to gift the assets of their estate, the decision against Harry Robert McCorkill's neo-Nazi will shows there are limits in Canada to whom you can leave your money as well as for what purpose.

10

RELIGION

What to do if a person puts religious stipulations for beneficiaries in their will and the designated beneficiaries object? Below are some examples.

Resurrection Will

A tenet of Jehovah's Witnesses is that "144,000 of Jesus's most faithful followers will be resurrected to rule with Jesus after the Earth is destroyed." Peter Tucker, a member who died on February 2, 1990, had believed he would be among the resurrected and return to his home and farm in Virden, Manitoba, following his death. Consequently, he wanted his thirty acres of land to be preserved for his use upon resurrection. At the time of signing his holographic will on December 10, 1988, he verbally declared his wish for his neighbour Fred Faucher to be the "caretaker" of his land but emphasized that nobody was to live in his house except his son, Lawrence. In his will he said Faucher should use the income from rent of a portion of his land "to pay all municipal land tax house fire insurance and Electricity that may become to be and cut all grass around the house" (Tucker didn't use commas).

He left his daughter, Lillian, "$1,000.00 one thousand dollars cash only" and bequeathed "the remaining assets cash and property to my son

Lawrence." He appointed Lawrence executor and trustee. Tucker was divorced, and Lillian lived with his ex-wife.

Faucher interpreted the will as giving him the right to the land for his lifetime. Lawrence Tucker interpreted it as giving him immediate possession of the property. Faucher said that at the time of the signing of the will, Peter Tucker had told him there was no time limit on how long he could have the land. Douglas Wardman, a neighbour who witnessed the will, said he was present when Peter made this promise. However, they had no written proof.

Faucher refused to budge. He took Lawrence Tucker to Manitoba's Court of Queen's Bench, which ruled in favour of Faucher. Displeased with this decision, Lawrence went to Manitoba's Court of Appeal, asking that it reverse the lower court's decision. A key issue was whether Peter's belief that he would be resurrected was "delusional" or "irrational" and therefore he lacked "testamentary capacity" when he made his will. In the preamble to his decision about what exactly Peter meant in his will, Manitoba Court of Appeal Justice David Kroft said, "Peter Tucker's acknowledged belief concerning resurrection was more literal than that held by traditional Jehovah's Witnesses. Without so finding or suggesting, I will assume that his extreme belief was so unfounded and illogical as to justify being described as an insane delusion." That said, the justice went on to say, "English and Canadian precedents make it quite clear that, according to the circumstances, a delusion may either undermine testamentary capacity or alternatively may have no effect upon the validity of a will."

Nobody had said Tucker wasn't of sound mind, Kroft said. Faucher and Wardman both agreed with Lawrence that Tucker managed his personal and business matters "knowledgeably, competently, and with success."

This was Justice Kroft's yardstick. It didn't matter what Peter's beliefs were; it only mattered that he had "testamentary capacity." He ruled in Lawrence's favour, saying, "It has never been denied that Lawrence Tucker is to be the ultimate beneficiary of the residue of his father's estate. My judgment means that he will receive his absolute interest in the land and farm sooner rather than later."

Finding a Loophole

Suppose your institution has been willed a wad of money, but to get it you would have to violate your firm stand against religious discrimination. What would you do? Would you outright reject the bequest, or would you try to find a loophole? Both a Prince Edward Island and a British Columbia university wriggled their way out of this challenge by finding a loophole. In one instance the money was for bursaries (based on financial need), in the other for scholarships (based on academic merit).

Eliza Jane Ramsden of Charlottetown, Prince Edward Island, who died in July 1994, left half her estate to the University of Prince Edward Island for scholarships to be named in honour of herself and her husband, who'd predeceased her. But there were strings attached regarding religion. Her will said: "These scholarships of a minimum of $1,000 and maximum of full tuition will be awarded to Protestant students who are in the greatest financial need. Academic achievement does not necessarily need to be a defining qualification. Preference to be given to students entering the field of ministry."

Her stipulation put the university in a quandary because it was non-denominational, and its regulations prohibited "the acceptance of gifts that prejudice our non-denominational character." Instead of flatly rejecting Ramsden's gift, the university went to PEI's Supreme Court hoping it could find a loophole. It did. In 1996, PEI Supreme Court Chief Justice K.R. MacDonald said it should get "a person or organization other than the university to administer the trust. There would be no ground of public policy then preventing the trust from taking effect." This was done and the scholarships still exist.

A somewhat similar situation arose from the will of Florence Gertrude McConnell of Victoria, British Columbia, who died in 1994, the same year as Ramsden. The chief difference was that she singled out Roman Catholics whereas Eliza Jane Ramsden selected Protestants. McConnell's will earmarked money to the University of Victoria to establish two bursaries for "practicing" Roman Catholic students, one in education and the other in music. The university went to the Supreme Court of British Columbia to find out if accepting the gift would violate the province's Human Rights Code and also "public policy against religious discrimination."

Justice Frank Maczko said it was all right to accept because "the relevant relationship was a private one between the testator and potential beneficiaries, not the university and its students. Being a private relationship, the Human Rights Code did not apply. The terms of the bursaries were not offensive to public policy merely because they restricted the class of potential recipients to members of a particular religious faith."

Mother's Wishes

On February 12, 1996, the *Toronto Star* showed a picture of a smiling Walter Fox sitting in his office, holding a picture of his late father, Ralph. Over Walter's left shoulder was a small piece of paper stuck to the wall that said in capital letters, "PEACE IS HERE." The *Star*'s caption read: "BITTER BATTLE: Walter Fox holds a picture of his father, Ralph, and a copy of a court judgment yesterday that said he could keep the inheritance his dad left him, which he lost when he married a non-Jew."

Ralph made his will in 1961. In it he appointed his wife, Miriam, as his sole executrix and gave her a life interest in 75 percent of the residue and Walter a life interest in the remaining 25 percent. If Walter survived his mother, upon her death he was to receive the residue. A "life interest" is a right to property that a person holds for life but can't dispose of further.

Walter got his law degree in 1967. In 1969, the same year Ralph died, Walter married a Jewish woman. Walter and his wife had two children from this marriage, a son, Ralph James, and a daughter, Shayne Melissa. Both children were brought up Jewish and were close to their grandmother, a devout adherent of Jewish beliefs and traditions.

Ralph's estate, primarily consisting of real estate, was valued at $750,000. It included his and Miriam's home, a share in a downtown Toronto apartment building, and a summer vacation cottage at Lake Simcoe, an hour's drive north of Toronto.

In 1984, fifteen years after Ralph's death, Walter and his wife separated. Ralph James stayed with his father for a while, then joined his sister, Shayne Melissa, at Grandmother Miriam's house. Over the next two years there was considerable litigation as to whether Ralph was paying support to the children on time, as called for in the separation agreement, or was delinquent, which his estranged wife maintained. It was a bitter battle. The divorce was finalized in 1986.

Walter became romantically involved with his long-time secretary, a Gentile. In April 1989, they decided to marry. When Walter told Miriam, who was among those Jews who oppose intermarriage with someone of a different faith, she was very upset.

Intermarriage is prohibited by the Torah, the Jewish scriptures. In Deuteronomy 7:3–4, God says: "Do not give your daughters to their sons or take their daughters for your sons for they will turn your children away from following me to serve other gods, and the Lord's anger will kindle against you and will quickly destroy you."

The Talmud, a commentary on the teachings of the Torah, says a marriage between a Jew and non-Jew doesn't constitute a marriage under Jewish law. The non-Jew would need to convert to Judaism in order for the marriage to be legal.

If a Jewish son marries a Gentile, their children aren't considered Jewish. If a Jewish daughter marries a non-Jew, the concern is that their children won't be practising Jews, although they will be considered Jewish because their mother is.

Particularly among Orthodox Jews, a son marrying a non-Jew is considered a sin. They cast him out by sitting shiva, seven days of mourning for a deceased, and say, "I have no son."

Ralph's will had given Miriam the power to sell off parts of his estate — "encroach" on it, in legalese — for the benefit of their grandchildren, should any be born. When Walter told his mother that he was going to marry a non-Jew, as punishment she both rewrote her will to disinherit him and, using the power she had as executrix of her late husband's estate, rerouted Walter's 25 percent life interest to his children. "You're not lawfully entitled to do this," Walter in his persona as a lawyer declared. He applied to the Ontario Superior Court, which deals with will disputes along with a broad range of other lawsuits, to stop her.

When the Ontario Superior Court said the will had given Miriam the "discretion" to do as she saw fit, Walter appealed upward to the Ontario

Court of Appeal. It gave its decision on February 7, 1996, the opposite of what the lower court had decided. Justice Patrick Gallagher wrote:

> That her son intended to marry a gentile was completely extraneous to the duty which the will obviously imposed upon Miriam, namely, to be concerned about the welfare of her grandchildren....
>
> I am of the view that in this case it would be contrary to public policy to permit a trustee effectively to disinherit the residual beneficiary because he dared to marry outside the religious faith of his mother. While decisions in the past upheld discriminatory conditions in wills, counsel in this case were not prepared to argue that any court would today uphold a condition in a will which provides that a beneficiary is to be disinherited if he or she marries outside of a particular religious faith. I find compelling the argument that if a testator could not do so then his trustee could not do it for him.

In fact, not only did the judge rule in Walter's favour; he also removed Miriam as the executrix of Raph's estate "as a result of her improper dealing with the assets."

Land Control

Clause 4 in the will of Thomas Allan Peach of Nova Scotia read: "My property at 89 Brookland St., Glace Bay is to be sold to an Anglican of [*sic*] Presbyterian and the amount placed in the balance of my estate" ("of" was a typo, changed by the court to "or"). Peach, who died in April 2009 at the age of ninety-four, had been a long-time congregant at St. Mary's Anglican Church in Glace Bay and had at one time studied for the ministry.

Justice A. David McAdam of the Supreme Court of Nova Scotia ruled in November 2009 that the will was "clearly discriminatory. It is in violation of section 5 of The Nova Scotia Human Rights Act which prohibits discrimination in the purchase or sale of real property on account of religion.

Therefore, the sale of Peach's property is not to be restricted to purchasers who are 'Anglican' or 'Presbyterian.'"

In the eyes of the law, religion shouldn't be used as a weapon.

11

GENDER EQUALITY

Does a will written in Canada have to be in sync with Canada's belief that women should have equality with men if the person writing it is from a culture that believes women are secondary to men?

This contentious issue is spotlighted by the mirror wills of Richmond, British Columbia, residents Nahar Singh Litt, who died February 2, 2016, age eighty-eight, and his wife, Nihal Kaur Litt, who died March 22, 2016, age eighty-nine. The Litts left 93.4 percent of their $9.3 million estate to their two sons to split ($4.2 million each) and 6.6 percent to their four daughters to subdivide ($150,000 each). Saying they were "victims of gender discrimination because their parents, of East Indian origin, adhered to East Indian customs and traditions that favour sons over daughters," the four daughters jointly applied to British Columbia's Supreme Court to have the wills "varied" (changed) to give them equal amounts to their brothers.

They were trailblazers. Trevor Todd, their lawyer, commented, "Over the course of my 45-year practice, I've had many Indo-Canadian women consult with me over wills they believe to be unfair. But none proceeded with a claim. The social pressures, family pressures, and pressure from their community at large prevented them from going ahead."

The brothers agreed that their sisters had been treated unfairly and should get greater amounts but opposed equal amounts because the "testamentary autonomy of the Parents should be respected."

The parents had created a "mirror will," which contains provisions that mirror those in another person's will. A common example is when each spouse or long-time partner creates a will that leaves everything to the other with the estate to go to their children when the surviving spouse or partner dies.

The Litts were Sikhs. So far as the scriptural value system of Sikhs is concerned, a woman has equal religious, social, economic, and political rights and she can hold political office. However, gender equality has been difficult to achieve in practice due to centuries-old social, cultural, and caste-related biases.

The Litts had been farmers in the northwest Indian state of Punjab, where the Sikh religion originated. Nihal had no formal education and Nahar had left school at the end of grade 7. They immigrated to British Columbia in 1964 and settled in an area of Vancouver that had a thriving Sikh community, one of the oldest and largest in Canada.

Nahar and Nihal had six children — sons Mukhtiar (Terry) and Kasar, and daughters Jasbinder, Mohinder, Inderjit, and Amarjit. The children were in their early teens or younger when the family came to Canada. Nahar found work at a sawmill, common for male Sikh newcomers to the province, and remained employed there until he retired in 1991, twenty-seven years later. A year after they arrived, Nahar and Nihil were able to afford to buy a house of their own and began to acquire others to rent out. They lived very frugally in order to save money to purchase more property.

As soon as they were old enough, the children were expected to work during the summers alongside their mother, picking fruit and vegetable crops on local farms. In accordance with Sikh beliefs, everyone, whether son or daughter, was expected to do the same kind of work and to work equally hard. Jasbinder recalled that her first job in Canada was picking potatoes with her mother for seventy cents an hour.

Nahar used his earnings from the sawmill and rents from homes in Vancouver he and Nihal acquired to finance the purchase of farmland in the

Vancouver area that the family personally worked on. Over the years Nahar bought more and more farmland. By the end of 1980, through the corporate entity Litt Farms, he owned five farm properties, totalling 185 acres, located in the Vancouver area at Abbotsford and Richmond. The biggest was eighty-acre Cambie Farm, bought in 1980 for $1,575,000. Real estate was Nahar and Nihal's, and later the estate's, most valuable asset. When Nahar and Nihal wrote their wills in 1993, their assets, primarily property, were worth between $2.5 million and $3.5 million. Inflation and their prime locations tripled the properties' value in the nearly quarter century until Nahar's and Nihal's deaths in 2016. Mohinder recalled, "My father told me that the land was 'a brick of gold.'"

At the trial everyone agreed that, growing up, work on the farms was hard; that the family had little money to spare and lived very frugally; that Nihal was a difficult and at times very mean person, especially toward her elder daughters; that both parents were strict; and that as adults when they were given cash as gifts toward buying a house or investing in property, sons Terry and Kasar received significantly more than the daughters.

For example, in 1993, Nahar provided cash to Jasbinder, Mohinder, Terry, and Kasar to allow them jointly to purchase an investment property. But the amounts were unequal. Sisters Jasbinder and Mohinder each received $10,000; brothers Terry and Kasar each received $50,000. Cash gifts to Terry alone were worth almost four times the gifts that the sisters collectively received.

The boys were never asked to clean the family's home nor help with meal preparation and service; these were duties assigned only to the girls, regarded traditionally in India as solely women's work. Amarjit recalled, "We daughters had no voice at home, and were controlled by our parents. The only way we received positive acknowledgment from them was 'for working hard and like men on the farms.' Life at home was based on our parents' traditional East Indian cultural views that boys are a blessing and girls a disappointment." Mohinder recalled being told by her mother: "You're lucky to have two brothers."

Nahar wouldn't let the girls join the school choir, track team, or other school activities, while Terry was allowed to play on the school hockey team and work on the school yearbook. The girls wore hand-me-down clothing; the boys were given expensive gifts, including a bike for Terry.

Nahar wouldn't allow Jasbinder to become a flight attendant; told Mohinder that if she didn't break off a relationship with a male student at the University of British Columbia and drop out of university, she'd be disowned; and forbade Inderjit from becoming a police officer. He did permit her to become a data-entry clerk at a hospital but insisted that she hand over a large portion of her earnings to the family's farming business.

The children's marriages were arranged by their parents in negotiations with families in India. When Inderjit refused to marry the man her parents had picked out for her, Nahar didn't speak to her for a year. As was the custom in India, Nahar and Nihal expected their married offspring, their spouses, and their children to live at "Family Quarters," Nahar's and Nihal's home. Nahar and Nihal didn't charge rent, but the daughters and daughters-in-law had to do all the household drudgery for the extended family. When Amarjit became pregnant by a Caucasian man and moved in with him, Nahar and Nihal cut off all communication with her, effectively disowning her.

Until a child married, their income was to go into the farming operations, essentially as a loan. Terry explained: "Without it and without the money Nahar was contributing from his income working at the sawmill, there wasn't enough income being earned from the operations to keep going."

Nahar and Nihil wrote their mirror wills in December 1993. The wills didn't explain their reasons for giving the bulk to the boys, nor did they write an accompanying explanatory document.

Terry was told the terms and ordered not to tell his siblings. Kasar later said that Nahar told him the contents in 1996. None of the daughters knew about the contents until after their parents' deaths.

Nahar executed a will in India in 1994 and another in 2006, both of which contradicted the 1993 wills he and Nihal had done. In both he said, "I have not prepared any other will before this one." He didn't revoke the Canadian one. The Indian wills left the whole of his estate to Terry and Kasar to be divided equally, with nothing left to the daughters. In the 2006 will he said, "My four daughters are married. I have given their share in the form of dowry at their weddings."

As Terry recalled, after Nihal had a heart attack in 2006, he suggested to her and Nahar that they revise their wills to give the girls more. "I told them that I thought they were unfair to the girls, the wills would divide the family, and everyone would end up in court. I urged them for six years, from 2006 to 2012. At one point my father said he was open to changing his will, but my mother wasn't."

Nihal didn't tell Terry the reason for her refusal. Terry surmised, "She was extremely frugal. Her unwillingness to accept that things cost more in Canada than in India led to significant problems in attempting to organize much needed paid in-home care for both parents in 2015, the year before they died. She was uneducated and generally unaware of the family's finances. For someone as frugal as her, $150,000 may have represented a very substantial sum, and she may not have turned her mind to the fact that this, even multiplied by four, represented only a small percentage of the overall Estate."

Since the couple's intention was to have mirror wills, Nahar, too, left his will as it was.

In 2014 Nahar developed Alzheimer's disease. Nihal's heart condition was also a matter of concern. They continued to live in their home, and the children found managing the many facets of their care extremely challenging. (The estrangement between the parents and Amarjit had ended by now and she was again part of the family fold.) The problems were exacerbated by Nihal's unyielding resistance to hiring outside help, her always abrasive personality becoming even more belligerent, and Nahar's Alzheimer's disease becoming more pronounced. Their relationship with each other seriously degenerated, creating one more thing for the children to attend to and manage.

The daughters, especially Mohinder and Jasbinder, took on most of the daily care and assistance the parents required, including meal preparation, personal care, and household chores. They found it overwhelming and stressful. Terry looked after financial matters on the parents' behalf and made sure that bills were paid. From time to time, he paid bills out of his own pocket.

Kasar, who lived next door to the parents, was largely uninvolved. The sisters, who were generally of one mind, frequently disagreed and argued with Terry, sometimes heatedly, about what should be done. Often, when Terry's suggestions were rejected, he simply withdrew, which generated more conflict.

Nihal was admitted to hospital on February 2, 2016, and the same day Nahar died at home. Nihal passed away on March 22, 2016.

By this time, the children were all in their fifties or sixties. They all were financially independent and in good health. None of them asserted a needs-based claim against the estate. On the other hand, there were significant disparities in income. Terry was the most well off financially by a substantial margin; Jasbinder, Kasar, and Amarjit the least.

The case was heard in February 2019 by British Columbia Supreme Court — Vancouver Justice Elaine J. Adair. Typically, courts don't easily permit the last wishes of a will-maker to be altered after their demise, only doing so in very specific circumstances where correcting injustice is the sole purpose. However, the British Columbia Wills Variation Act does allow judges to change a will to make sure it's "adequate, just and equitable" to the testator's spouse and children. In addition, BC courts don't uphold wills that demonstrate sexual orientation and gender expression bias, preferential gender treatment, or cultural inequities that are not societal norms in British Columbia or that have racial overtones.

Justice Adair issued her decision July 17, 2019. "I give little weight to the Indian wills," she said referring to the wills Nahar had written in India in 1994 and 2006. "There are too many inconsistencies with other reliable evidence."

Then she got to the heart of the matter. She was nuanced:

> I am not persuaded that, in making the Wills, the Parents considered themselves bound [underlining by Justice Adair] by East Indian cultural traditions, and I reject the argument that the Parents' reasons for dividing the Estate in the way reflected in the Wills were driven solely by adherence to those traditions. The Wills themselves — in particular, the gift to Amarjit, the daughter the Parents had disowned when the Wills were made — show the

> Parents did not consider themselves so bound. Rather, in my view, the Parents' reasons for dividing the Estate in the way reflected in the Wills are more complicated. Assuming (as the Daughters ask me to do) that the Parents felt bound by East Indian cultural tradition to divide the Estate in a particular way itself reflects stereotypical thinking about what "traditional" East Indian parents would do.
>
> I agree with Mr. Lee [Terry's lawyer] that for Nihal in particular, a cash gift of $150,000 is likely to have seemed a very substantial sum. It was Nihal who was not open to changing the Wills when Terry raised it with the Parents. Nahar, on the other hand, was. This evidence is incompatible with the conclusion that the Parents felt themselves bound by culture to divide the Estate in a way that effectively disinherited the Daughters.
>
> On the other hand, looking at the whole of the evidence, I have concluded that traditional cultural values had some influence on the Parents in how they treated the Siblings, both when the Parents were alive and in the Wills. Although Kasar did not fare as well as Terry and often clashed with Nahar over money, in the Litt family, there was never equality of treatment between the Sons and the Daughters.

This said, she carefully threaded the needle in her decision between the old and the new mindsets. She rejected the daughters' wish for equal amounts with their brothers while on the other hand substantially increasing the amount they should get. Her opinion was that both the old and the new could be respected. She said,

> Given the size of the Estate, there can be a significant increase in the size of the gifts to the Daughters, without repudiating altogether the Parents' testamentary autonomy. In my view, equal division of the Estate is not the only fair result.

> Based on the factors discussed above, particularly the gifts and benefits that the Sons received during the Parents' lifetimes, the influence of cultural values on the Parents' choices, and the Daughters' contributions to the Parents' care, I have concluded that there needs to be a substantial increase in the gifts to the Daughters. However, as discussed above, I have not been persuaded that the Parents' choice not to treat all Siblings equally should be rejected as motivated solely by unacceptable discrimination against daughters.
>
> In my view, the provision that is adequate, just, and equitable in the circumstances in view of the Parents' moral obligations to the Daughters, and that respects (to the appropriate degree) the Parents' testamentary autonomy, is to divide the Estate 60% in favour of the Daughters and 40% in favour of the Sons. The Daughters' 60% share will be divided equally among the four of them, and the Sons' 40% share will be divided equally among the two of them.

That meant the four daughters as a group got $5.4 million of the $9 million estate, each with an individual portion of $1.35 million, and the two sons combined got $3.6 million, or $1.8 million each. The daughters had won their argument that they should get much more, and the sons had won their argument that they still should get more each than each daughter. Terry had argued that the sisters receive amounts based on each one's needs, but Justice Adair preferred equal amounts in keeping with the overarching objective of equality.

"All my sisters and I are happy with the judge's finding," Amarjit told reporters. "We are still able to honour our parents' wishes that the sons get more but there's more fairness now." Contesting the parents' will wasn't easy, she said, especially for her two older sisters. "We did it because it was the right thing to do," she said, adding that she hoped their case "will inspire other women in the same situation to stand up for themselves."

12

MORAL OBLIGATION

Does a parent have a moral obligation, a moral duty, to leave "adequate" money to their spouse and children in their will? It depends on where you live and a judge's point of view. There is neither uniformity nor unanimity.

The idea that there is a moral obligation has gained momentum since a 1994 decision by the Supreme Court of Canada, *Tataryn v. Tataryn*, but it's fuzzy as to when and how it applies as the examples in this chapter show. British Columbia and Ontario had moral obligation will rules long before the Supreme Court weighed in, and they remain the only provinces to have such rules. However, their rules differ. For example, British Columbia's apply to adult as well as young children, while Ontario's don't include adult children.

The Baby Boom generation, those born between 1946 and 1965, is about 25 percent, 9.2 million, of Canada's population, and there are 2.9 million folks over age seventy-five, according to Statistics Canada. They're on their final stretch, which means there's going to be a large intergenerational transfer of money via wills in the near future — some estimates say about $1 trillion. With so much money at stake, it's inevitable that fights will break out over estates, and there will be a big increase in court cases. It's also inevitable that the issue of "moral obligation" will be the focus because it's such an amorphous term, unlike the explicitness of legal obligation regulations, and therefore lends itself to broad interpretation.

Landmark *Tataryn v. Tataryn* Case

"I always loved my husband and respected him, and I would never do anything wrong to him, and I did exactly what he wanted me to do, and I just can't understand this," Mary Tataryn said in bewilderment about her husband Alexander's ("Alex") will when it was opened following his death February 24, 1989, at age sixty-nine.

She decided to challenge the will, and the unexpected result was a whole new perspective by the Supreme Court of Canada impacting all of Canada on what a will should ideally do regarding the treatment of immediate family. The court said that "moral obligation" should supersede "testamentary freedom" when immediate family can show it has been unfairly treated.

Mary contested Alex's will under section 2(1) of the British Columbia Wills Variation Act, which had been passed seventy years earlier, in 1920. The wording in 1989 when Mary went to court and today is the same as it was in 1920 — that is, it states that if the testator fails to make adequate provision for the proper maintenance and support of a surviving spouse and children, the court may order the provision from the estate that it considers "adequate, just and equitable in the circumstances." The wording lacks clarity, and how it was interpreted has changed and broadened over the years.

In the 1920s, courts interpreted the act as only requiring provision for basic needs and maintenance to avoid a surviving spouse and children becoming a public charge upon the country (i.e., avoid welfare). In the 1930s courts extended their interpretation beyond necessities to the more generous "preservation of standard of living" based on overall societal opinion of what that should be. That, too, could be construed in conflicting ways; for instance, "adequate and proper" can mean different things depending on the size of an estate. A small bequest might not be considered "adequate and proper" if an estate is large.

The lack of clarity resulted in many disputes over "adequate and proper" flooding the courts. The most significant remains the Supreme Court's 1994 decision regarding Mary Tataryn that made crystal clear why and when moral obligation should be taken into account.

Alex Tataryn, a shoemaker, and his wife, Mary, who'd been a waitress, lived in Prince George, British Columbia. At the time of Alex's death, they'd been married for forty-three years and had two sons, John and Edward. Elder son John was living with his parents in their home and younger son Edward in New Brunswick when Alex died. Alex's estate was valued at $315,264.49. It consisted of the house he, Mary, and John lived in, a rental property inherited from Alex's father, and their bank accounts.

Alex and Mary hadn't discussed the subject of death. They thought they were both in good health and that there was no need yet to talk about wills. Mary recalled: "I knew he had money, but I never questioned him about it, and I thought, well, it is for our old age. I didn't care. I trusted my husband. We had an agreement that we were going to keep the house going and he was going to save for our old age, so we always used to put his money in the bank."

Alex disliked John to the point that not only did he leave him out of the will, but he also structured the will in such a way that Mary wouldn't be able to give any of the estate to John. He created a life estate for his wife in the matrimonial home and made her the beneficiary of a discretionary trust, with Edward as trustee. The will stipulated that after her death, everything would go to Edward.

Alex explained in clause 4 of his will:

> I HAVE PURPOSELY excluded my son, JOHN ALEXANDER TATARYN, from any share of my Estate and purposely provided for my wife by the trust as set out above for the following reason: My wife MARY and my older son JOHN have acted in various ways to disrupt my attempts to establish harmony in the family. Since JOHN was 12 years old he has been a difficult child for me to raise. He has turned against me and totally ignored me for the last 15 years of his life. He has been abusive to the point of profanity; he has been extremely inconsiderate and has

> made no effort to reconcile his differences with me. He has never been open to discussion with a view to establishing ourselves in unity. My son EDWARD is respectable, and I commend him for his warm attitude towards me, his honesty, and his co-operation with me.

At trial court the judge revoked the gift of the house next door to Edward and granted Mary a life interest in it, directed that John and Edward each receive an immediate gift of $10,000 out of the residue of the estate, and ordered that when Mary died, the residue of the estate be divided one-third to John and two-thirds to Edward. John and Edward accepted the decision, but Mary didn't because the judge had left in place Edward's control over her. She regarded this as unwarranted and unacceptable and went to the BC Court of Appeal to get this erased. The court turned her down. She soldiered on, proceeding to the top of the judicial hierarchy, the Supreme Court of Canada, where the case was heard on May 3, 1994. Its decision, given July 14, 1994, was a complete victory for Mary. She was now in the superior position and Edward subordinate. "Life interest" in the matrimonial home was replaced with "title" (ownership). She got life interest in the next-door property, which had been earmarked for Edward in Alex's will. The trial judge's ruling that each son immediately get $10,000 from the residue of the estate wasn't changed. Neither John nor Edward had protested the amount.

Mother's Obligation

Pacita Gutkowski, seventy-three, died December 26, 2021, at Royal Columbian Hospital, New Westminster, British Columbia. In her will she left 25 percent of her $881,000 estate to her son, Nicolas, her only child, and divided the remaining 75 percent between her sister, Dolores Laigo, and her niece, Rosalie Olbinado. Nicolas felt he should get more and Dolores and Rosalie less. He went to British Columbia's Supreme Court seeking more for "moral obligation" reasons.

Pacita was born on May 27, 1948, in Luna, La Union, Philippines. She was the eldest of eleven children — six boys and five girls. She was unmarried in 1976 when she had a son, whom she named Nicolas Bautista.

When he was three months old, she left him with his grandparents in the Philippines and moved to Canada to work as a nanny.

In Canada, Pacita married Adam Gutkowski. She was employed at the Catholic Sisters of the Cenacle at their Shaughnessy, Vancouver, location until it closed in 1998. She then joined the Oblates of Mary Immaculate in Vancouver as a cook, retiring in 2015 following the death of her husband.

Nicolas didn't see his mother from the time she left until he was seven. They then met every three to four years after that. Pacita contributed some money to him for his education and living expenses but told him she couldn't do more because "living in Canada is hard." Still, by dint of hard work and saving, she accumulated quite a large estate of $881,000 by the time of her death.

Nicolas accused Dolores and Rosalie of driving a wedge between him and his mother by mischaracterizing him as a womanizer and lazy good-for-nothing. He also charged that they deliberately kept him uninformed about his mother's deteriorating health "in the hope that I would not benefit from her estate."

He challenged the will under section 60 of the British Columbia Wills, Estates and Succession Act, which was passed on October 29, 2009, and came into force on March 31, 2014. It incorporated the terms of the 1920 Wills Variation Act. As section 2(1) of that act had, section 60 says a court can vary a will to provide more adequate provision for a spouse or child if the will is deemed to be unfair.

In wills variation cases, the court will consider estrangement as a factor when assessing the strength of a moral obligation claim. In a number of cases, the court determined that a period of estrangement between the will-maker and their adult child negated the moral duty or obligation owed by the will-maker, undercutting the child's claim to vary the will. Courts have been more likely to arrive at this conclusion if the estrangement continues without reconciliation up to the death of the will-maker.

However, even among cases of unreconciled estrangements, not all are equal. Unlike in the family law context where blame for the breakdown of a relationship is not a relevant consideration, the court does consider who is at fault for an estrangement in the context of wills variation cases. For adult children, if the decision to cut off contact was initiated or perpetuated by the will-maker, the court may not consider the estrangement to negate the moral obligation owed to the adult child. This was the view taken by British Columbia's Supreme Court in Nicolas's request that his mother's will be varied in his favour.

It accepted as "facts" that Pacita had "abandoned" Nicolas as a three-month-old baby, had failed to move him to Canada to be with her once she was financially able to do so, and chose to be estranged from him later in life despite his attempts to build a relationship, but it said his allegations of misconduct by his aunt and cousin were just "hearsay."

The court pointed out that Pacita herself had acknowledged her moral obligation to her son by providing him with a 25 percent share in her estate.

Referring to the 1994 decision of the Supreme Court of Canada in the Tataryn case as a yardstick, the British Columbia Supreme Court said moral obligation should take precedence over testamentary autonomy in this case, and therefore it was "varying" Pacita's will to provide Nicolas with 60 percent of her estate, with the aunt and cousin each receiving 20 percent rather than their previously combined 75 percent.

Father's Obligation

In his will, Ronald Maurice Poole, who died on October 10, 2017, in Surrey, British Columbia, disinherited his only children, thirty-four-year-old twin daughters Courtney and Chelsea, whom he'd had in a non-marital relationship, and left his entire estate to two friends, Bernard Allen Sabiston and Ian Campbell Toombs. The daughters went to the British Columbia Supreme Court to get his will varied. At trial, the issues were:

> (a) Did Poole owe a moral obligation to the twins to provide for them?
> (b) If so, how much should they get from his estate?

The troubling story began when Ronald was thirty-four. After divorcing his first wife, he started dating twenty-three-year-old Celine LeBlanc, and she became pregnant. When Celine informed him of her pregnancy, he raised the possibility of an abortion. Celine rebuffed the suggestion. The twins were born on January 13, 1986. Ronald and Celine never married, nor did they live together in a marriage-like relationship. Celine raised the twins as a single mother without any involvement or financial assistance from Ronald.

When the twins were ten months old, Celine took them from Edmonton, Alberta, where they'd been living, and moved to Hay River, Northwest Territories. Celine met and developed a close friendship with Bill and Gloria Fandrick and their family. In June 1988, Celine prepared her will appointing the Fandricks as the twins' joint guardians on her death. She also took out a $100,000 life insurance policy on her life naming the twins as the beneficiaries. She died on February 1, 1990, of pneumonia complications. Her daughters were then four. On her death, the insurance proceeds were placed in trust with the territory's Public Guardian and Trustee Office because the children were minors.

The day following Celine's death, her mother, Dianna Coull, notified the Fandricks that she intended to seek custody of the twins. Ronald then filed suit to become the custodial parent as their "natural father." He proposed that Coull help raise them. He met his daughters for the first time when he travelled to Yellowknife in May 1990 for an extended visit in advance of the start of the trial in September. They began calling him "Daddy."

The custody trial was in Yellowknife before the Supreme Court of the Northwest Territories, Justice Mary Elizabeth Noonan presiding. At the trial Poole said he was prepared to permanently settle in Yellowknife.

However, when Justice Noonan handed down her decision on December 13, 1990, she appointed Gloria and Bill Fandrick as the twins' custodial parents. In her reasons, the justice commented:

> It is clear that Mr. Poole had little or no contact with Celine after the twins were born and he did not see his daughters until May 1990. He says he tried to contact Celine on several occasions without success. I must say I was not convinced that he made an assertive attempt to meet his parental responsibilities.

Noonan gave Poole and Coull generous in-person access to the twins plus telephone access and consultations by the Fandricks about education, health, recreational pursuits, and other major areas of the twins' lives.

Angry and bitter about the decision, Poole left Yellowknife, dropped out of the twins' lives, and disappeared. He married a second time; he and his wife didn't have children, and he divorced her. Despite never being prevented by the Fandricks from seeing the girls, Poole didn't exercise any of the parenting time that was granted. Nor did he ever provide any financial assistance to the Fandricks for the twins. The couple relied on their own resources and a $350 per month allowance paid to them by the Public Trustee from the twins' trust funds.

The one exception to Poole making no effort to contact his daughters was in 1991, the year following the Noonan order, when he reached out through a lawyer asking if they could visit him in Vancouver because his mother (and the twins' grandmother, whom they had never met) was dying. The Fandricks had concerns about exposing the then-five-year-old twins to another traumatic situation involving death because of what they had experienced with Celine and said no.

On May 20, 1995, five years after losing the custody trial and when the twins were nine years old, Poole prepared a will ("First Will") naming his sister as beneficiary and explicitly disinheriting the twins, referring to them as "my illegitimate children." The First Will stated:

> I have no desire to benefit my illegitimate children even if my sister … predeceases me, as they are well taken care of and I have absolutely no contact or association with them.

When the twins became adults, the Fandricks gave them a box containing the court documents, affidavits, and transcripts of the custody trial. Courtney and Chelsea were shocked and upset at the revelation that Poole had suggested to Celine that they be aborted.

Poole made a second will dated October 2, 2006, when Courtney and Chelsea were age twenty, again explicitly disinheriting them:

> My two children, Chelsea and Courtney not be included in this my Will due to the following reasons:
>
> a) That they have not made any efforts to see me, contact me or even make me aware of their circumstances as they may be from time to time;
>
> b) That they have been well looked after through their Mother's Estate in the form of a $100,000 trust fund.... They should not need any further assistance from me, though I do still miss them and realize that the choice of where to live was not theirs.

This will ordered Bernard Allen Sabiston and Ian Campbell Toombs, who were appointed executors and trustees and who were the sole beneficiaries of the residuary of his estate, to block any attempt by Courtney and Chelsea to apply to vary it, authorizing them to deplete the entire capital of the estate, if need be, to do so:

> If this will is contested, I direct my trustees to litigate such contest and I authorize my trustees to encroach upon all the assets of my estate and all of the funds and resources therefrom in their entirety to litigate such a contest and to strenuously litigate such a contest.

At the time of Poole's death a decade later, his estate was valued at $879,174.42. Chelsea, now married, was working at a car dealership and had little significant savings or assets. For the past eleven years, she had suffered from a debilitating medical condition known as myasthenia gravis, a chronic autoimmune disease that affects the communication between nerves and muscles. The disease's ongoing symptoms made it difficult for Chelsea to work routine hours.

Her sister, Courtney, was a full-time primary school teacher. Additionally, she cared for underprivileged and Indigenous children as a foster mother, five or more at a time. Also married, she and her husband were just slightly better off financially than Chelsea.

Bernard Sabiston and Ian Toombs, Ronald Poole's designated beneficiaries, were seventy-two and seventy-four, respectively, and both described themselves as financially independent.

The court's judgment was given by Justice G.P. (Gary) Weatherill on April 17, 2021. In his preliminary remarks the justice slammed Poole:

> The Deceased's rationale for disinheriting the Twins is, I conclude, invalid, irrational, and not based on what a reasonable testator judged by contemporary community standards would or should have done. Indeed, the comments made about the Twins in both wills were unwarranted, cruel, and untrue. They were not what a judicious father in these circumstances discharging his moral duty to his children would have said or done, especially considering the Twins' difficult upbringing, and considering they were the only persons he owed a moral duty to.
>
> Messrs. Sabiston and Toombs both said that they felt a moral obligation to strenuously oppose the Twins' application because of the Deceased's comments. As the executors of the Deceased's estate, they are required to remain neutral. It is, therefore, disingenuous of them to suggest they are strenuously contesting this action on the basis of a "moral" obligation to the Deceased, as that obligation is void.
>
> I conclude that the Deceased abandoned the Twins from the outset and he had a strong moral obligation to attempt to make up for his desertion of them in the Second Will. He owed a moral obligation to them and failed to meet it during his lifetime. Messrs. Sabiston and Toombs' moral claim to the Deceased's estate, if they even have one, pales by comparison to that of the Twins.

This all said, he gave his decision: "Accordingly, I am varying the Second Will in order that it make adequate, just and equitable provision for the Twins while at the same time interferes as little as possible with the Deceased's autonomy and expressed intentions."

The girls had suggested that if the court ruled in their favour they would like "a global award," which they would divide between them as they saw fit. Weatherill said, "As virtuous as that approach may seem on first blush, it could lead to discord and disharmony between them which must be discouraged."

He apportioned 35 percent each to Courtney and Chelsea and 15 percent each to Sabiston and Toombs.

He wasn't through. He proceeded to give his opinion of Poole. It was harsh, deserved.

> The Deceased lost the battle for custody and thereafter, through bitterness, stubbornly decided to blame them. He put what he felt was in his own best interests first and was not prepared to accept Justice Noonan's ruling that it was in the Twins' best interests that they stay with the Fandricks.
>
> The fact that he made it so clear in the First Will and the Second Will that the Twins were illegitimate, that he wanted no part of his estate to go to them, and instructed his executors to fight any attempt by them to vary his will, speaks volumes about his attitude towards them and his misguided and ill-conceived attempt to punish them for matters beyond their control. Despite being granted very generous parenting time, he failed and/or neglected to exercise any parenting time or to have anything further to do with his own children.
>
> He failed in his last opportunity to behave like a judicious father and recognize in the Second Will his moral obligations to the Twins.

The rejection of Poole's twisted, vindictive thinking spotlights that disinheritance legally must have "valid and rational reasons" and not be motivated by spite.

Sisters

Tat Kuan Cheong of Richmond, British Columbia, died April 22, 2021, two months after writing a will in which he told a big fat lie. He had had three daughters, Cheong Chan "Celina," Hang Cheong "Ina," and Man Cheong "Sophia," but in the will he described Celina as his niece and left her $10,000 compared to the $340,000 residue from his $730,000 estate to be split between Ina and Sophia, whom he called his daughters in his will. Celina went to British Columbia's Supreme Court saying that Tat Kuan had failed to perform his "moral obligation" to her as her parent. Ina and Sophia protested that Celina shouldn't get more. It was their latest act of animosity toward Celina, stemming from their hatred and jealousy of her since they were children.

The girls were all born in Macau, China — Celina in 1951, Ina in 1953, and Sophia in 1955. Tat Kuan held three jobs but still had trouble making ends meet. His solution was to hand over Celina to his sister Kan "Kit Gee" and her husband Kan Chik Yin, a wealthy businessman living in Hong Kong, for the couple to raise. They were willing because they were childless. They never tried to adopt her.

Justice Lisa A. Warren, who wrote the court's decision, commented about Tat Kuan's action:

> On all accounts, Tat Kuan was a kind and loving man. Celina testified that he later told her he gave away her young self in order to create her adult self, implying that he thought that it was in her interests to be raised as the daughter of Kit Gee and Chik Yin. Sophia testified that when she was in her late teens or early twenties, Tat Kuan told her he gave Celina up to provide her with a better life. I accept that Tat Kuan acted with good intentions, but his intentions do not alter the reality of the consequences of his decision. I accept Celina's evidence that being abandoned by her father and told to treat Kit Gee and Chik Yin as if they were her parents was very confusing for her, and caused her immense emotional pain that has remained throughout her life.

As Ina and Sophia saw it, Celina as the eldest child had been given a better life than they had. The house Celina lived in was spacious, with modern amenities (including plumbing, hot water, and appliances), servants' quarters, and a large yard and garden. She had her own air-conditioned bedroom, stylish clothing, and lots of toys. She attended private school.

A few years after dispatching Celina, Tat Kuan had sent Ina to live with his mother, who dwelled in Macau. However, Ina's lifestyle was markedly different from Celina's. The grandmother's home was a two-bedroom apartment, without flush toilets, hot water, a refrigerator, or television. As many as seven or eight people lived there, and Ina had to share a bed with several cousins. Food was at times scarce. Sophia was the only one of Tat Kuan's daughters living with him and his second wife (Louise), and it was a very modest existence within a small studio apartment. Tat Kuan's older brother Tat Wai, who was physically disabled, also lived there.

While Ina and Sophia lived in straitened circumstances, Tat Kuan did manage to send them to pricey schools. He treated them fondly. Celina, however, lived in fear. Chik Yin was an alcoholic and screamed and yelled at night when he was drunk. He physically abused his wife, Kit Gee. Celina was constantly afraid he would beat her too.

Ina and Sophia remained hostile to Celina as the years passed. In 1987, Tat Kuan and Louise moved to British Columbia. Initially, they resided in an apartment owned by Ina, but they purchased an apartment in Richmond around 1990, where they lived for the rest of their lives.

In late 2020, Celina learned from Louise that Tat Kuan had lung cancer. She emailed Ina and Sophia, offering to share the cost of hiring a caregiver for him and Louise, who was also in failing health. Neither Ina nor Sophia replied. Celina phoned Tat Kuan and asked if he needed financial help and he told her he did not. He, Ina, and Sophia all told the lawyer drawing up his will that he only had two daughters and that Celina was his niece.

Louise died March 30, 2021, and Tat Kuan died three weeks later.

Ina organized his funeral. Neither she nor Sophia advised Celina, then living in the United States, of the arrangements. Celina learned about the timing of the funeral on the morning it was happening and managed to quickly arrange to have a rose delivered.

The death notice provided by Ina and Sophia to newspapers referred to Tat Kuan as having had only two daughters. Celina sent an email to both complaining about what she called "a distortion of the truth." Neither responded. A few weeks later, she sued over the will, saying her father had failed to meet his moral obligation to her.

The sisters were now financially better off than Celina, having made a lot of money in real estate. They opposed Celina getting more than she'd been willed. In her decision of September 9, 2024, Justice Warren sided with Celina, saying the will should be varied so that the three sisters each got the same sum.

13

FOUR HORSES

> I Direct and Declare that my Executors have my horses shot by the Royal Canadian Mounted Police and then buried.
>
> — CLIVE WISHART

Why had Clive Wishart, a New Brunswick farmer who lived alone, written this, considering that he'd rescued and adored the horses? Incredible as it may seem, he did it because he loved them and feared they'd be mistreated after he was gone. Clive's executors didn't want to obey his execution order, nor did the RCMP. People around the world sent letters pleading for the horses to be saved.

Clive lived in Tabusintac, northeast New Brunswick, a sparsely populated, unincorporated community. When he died on May 31, 1991, at age sixty-four, his draft horses — Jack, age nine; Bill and Barney, both seven; and King, five — were in good health, with an expected average lifespan of twenty-five to thirty years.

In Canada, unlike in the United States, animals cannot be named beneficiaries in a will on the basis that animals are property, and property can't inherit property. However, a provision can be made in a will for the establishment of a trust fund for the care of the animal, taking into account the usual lifespan of the breed, food and veterinarian costs, and the standard of care wanted. It's not a new trend for people to leave bequests to their pets over family and friends. For example, in 1835, a wealthy Englishman named Robert Mitford bequeathed the whole of his fortune in trust for the support of his string of horses, leaving his wife with zilch. British antiques dealer Ben Rea, who died in 1988, left £7 million (Can$12 million) to his cat, Blackie, and nothing to his relatives. Guinness World Records said the inheritance made Blackie "the wealthiest cat in the world."

Here in Canada, an Ottawa man, David Harper, who died in 2005 at age seven-nine, left a generous provision for his cat, Red. Harper, who was unmarried, childless, reclusive, and spent little on himself, had accumulated an estate worth $1.3 million at the time of his death. He left it all to the United Church of Canada with the stipulation that in exchange, the church would arrange to look after his sole companion, a three-year old tabby he had rescued.

"It's the first time I've worked out the details of a will involving a live animal," said Cynthia Gunn, the church's lawyer. "Mr. Harper wasn't a churchgoer. We're just glad he picked the United Church." Under the agreement, $80 a month was to be spent on the cat's care and feeding for the rest of its life. The church, dubbed in newspaper headlines as "The Church of Red," was also to cover the cat's veterinarian bills. Red would be getting good but not extravagant care.

Harper's neighbour, John Bell, told the *Ottawa Citizen* that Harper "had successive cats, all named Red. And they had to be orange tabbies." Harper, who worked in the public service as a gardener at Ottawa's Experimental Farm, loved flowers and animals. "He just saved," Bell told the *Citizen*. "He grew up in poverty and never spent any money. He made the same meal every day — chicken with two veg. He got his clothes at the Salvation Army.

"He would go out for a walk every morning at 5:30, and Red would walk along behind him."

Sometimes, as in Red's case, instructions in wills by pet owners are followed to the letter, in others, not. The most famous such instance is what happened to Trouble, the beloved white Maltese lapdog and chief companion of American multi-millionaire hotel owner Leona Helmsley. Leona, who died in 2007, left Trouble $12 million, the bulk of her estate. The general reaction worldwide was that this was excessive. Leona had been widely disliked, dubbed the "Queen of Mean" due to her mistreatment of her employees, and had served eighteen months in federal prison on tax evasion charges in the early 1990s.

Leona's relatives, whom she'd omitted from her will, were furious that they got nothing and the dog got everything. They went to court and the judge whittled down Trouble's inheritance to $2 million.

None of Leona's family nor acquaintances wanted the aptly named Trouble, who was known for biting everyone's fingers. Even restaurant waiters were said to have put on gloves as protection when Leona brought along the dog.

Following Leona's death, her brother had Trouble flown by private jet to the Helmsley Sandcastle hotel in Sarasota, Florida, where she was tended to around the clock. Her caretaker spent $100,000 annually on her care — including $8,000 for grooming and $1,200 for dog food. Four years later, and by this time blind, the world's richest lapdog passed away at the age of twelve.

In another case, Florida millionaire socialite Gail Posner, who died in 2010, bequeathed ownership and occupation of her mansion, valued at $8.4 million, and a $3 million trust fund to her three tiny dogs, Conchita, April Maria, and Lucia. The dogs each had their own luxury bedroom in the house and wardrobes for each season, slept in cashmere sweaters, wore expensive jewellery, had a personal hair stylist, and travelled in their own gold-coloured Cadillac Escalade to spa appointments. Household staff were willed $27 million in return for taking care of the dogs.

Posner left her son, from whom she'd been estranged for many years although they reconciled as she was dying, $1 million. He contested the will, alleging that the staff had exercised undue influence on his mother.

Whether ultra-rich like Helmsley and Posner or of modest income like the hard-saving David Harper and Clive Wishart, pet owners who are solitary or don't feel there's a suitable caregiver to take over are consumed with anxiety about the future of their pets after they die. It can work out well, but other times the trustee turns out to be a very bad choice, cruel to the animal, and pockets the money for their own use.

This is why the Clive Wisharts of this world resort to drastic measures. Generally, the animals are pet dogs and cats; Wishart's will was distinctive in that his pets were horses. It was also distinctive in that he wanted them shot. At one time horses who'd suffered a broken leg and had no chance of recovering were shot to death. Nowadays they're given a death-inducing injection.

Clive Wishart had bought his four draft horses, one Belgian and three Percherons, from a man who had entered them in controversial and gruelling agricultural fair hauling contests. While some people regarded the contests as sport, others, including Clive, saw it as abuse. In these contests, the prize goes to the horse that's fastest in hauling heavy loads equal to its weight, which is, on average, one ton. Clive provided his rescued horses sanctuary in a pasture at his farm, his daily highlight feeding them sugar cubes.

Clive's executors, relatives Myles and John Wishart, submitted the will for probate to the Probate Court of the Judicial District of Newcastle, New Brunswick, which includes Tabusintac. At the hearing, held between December 30 and 31, 1991, another relative, Max Wishart, tried to save the four horses by claiming Clive had lacked "testamentary capacity" — that is to say that he lacked the mental capacity to know what he was doing.

This tactic flopped, as many witnesses testified that Clive very much had testamentary capacity, and on the basis of their testimony, the presiding judge, Justice Thomas Riordan, admitted the will to probate on June 15, 1992. Myles and John then applied to the Court of Queen's Bench for "opinion, advice, and direction." Again, Justice Riordan presided. In legal terms the issue was which should prevail — testamentary freedom or public policy? Was the clause instructing the destruction of the animals against public policy / the public good and therefore should be invalidated?

Meanwhile, a neighbour, Lorne Harding, gave the animals refuge on his farm.

The filing with the court attracted intense national and international press attention. Lorne Harding and another Tabusintac resident, Marianne Palmer, started a letter-writing campaign urging that the court spare the horses. The court was inundated with letters from around the world pleading for the horses not to be executed. The New Brunswick Society for the

Prevention of Cruelty to Animals and the Canadian Federation of Humane Societies pitched in on behalf of the horses being allowed to live.

Riordan heard the case August 31, 1992, and gave his judgment a month later, on September 28. Conceivably, he could have quickly disposed of the case with a simple "Yes, it's against public policy" or "It's not" and a sentence, maybe two, of explanation. Instead, he gave it the full treatment, and it took quite a while for him to reach the finishing line.

He began with an observation:

> This direction to shoot four horses has resulted in a strong public protest of objection across the country. One can speculate that if the subject animals were pigs rather than horses, such opposition would not have been forthcoming. The horse is and always has been highly regarded by mankind and rightfully so.
>
> Wherever man has left his footprint in the long ascent from barbarism to civilization we find the footprint of the horse beside it. According to Western European mythology and folklore, all the great early civilizations arose among horse-owning, horse-breeding, and horse-using nations; those in which the horse was either unknown or in the feral, or untamed, state were backward, and no great forward movement of mankind was made without the assistance of the horse. So consistently was this the case that the glorified figure of "man on horseback" became the symbol of power. The image of the horse was stamped upon man's coinage, sculptured on his temples, and even worshipped as divine.
>
> Religious writing acknowledges the importance of the horse. One example is found in II Kings, chapter 2, verse 11 of the Holy Bible — "And it came to pass, as they still went on, and talked, that, behold, there appeared a chariot of fire, and horses of fire, and parted them both asunder; and Elijah went up by a whirlwind into heaven."

Riordan continued:

> Petitions to save the horses have been signed. Concerned citizens from both Canada and the United States have written to the court, to counsel, and to newspapers. Radio talk shows have debated the subject. One letter that demonstrates the interest that this has caused was posted from Vancouver to "The Judge, Tabusintac Court House, Tabusintac, New Brunswick" and is entirely in the elementary printing of a young child and is as follows:
>
> 4470 ANGUS VANCOUVER
> DEAR JUDGE, PLEASE DONT LET ANYONE KILL
> THE HORSES
> I LOVE HORSES BUT MY DAD WONT
> LET ME HAVE ONE.
> I WILL BE SAD IF THEY GET KILLED.
> FROM
> JENNIFER

But, the judge said, "The decision the court has a responsibility to make cannot be based on sentiment or public opinion but must be based on legal principles in accordance with the law of the land. He is not a knight-errant, roaming at will in pursuit of his own ideal of beauty or of goodness. He is to draw his inspiration from consecrated principles. He is not to yield to spasmodic sentiment, to vague and unregulated benevolence."

Riordan then trotted into the nub of the case: Should Barney, Bill, Jack, and King be put to death, or should the court intervene and render invalid the expressed direction of their now deceased owner?

> It is undisputed that Barney, Bill, Jack, and King were treated by Clive Wishart as pets; he was concerned with their welfare and did not want them to be abused. The solicitor who took instructions and prepared the will of Clive

> Wishart testified at the hearing of the Probate Court before me. That solicitor, Mr. William Munroe, was asked at that hearing why Clive Wishart directed that his horses be shot. It was his reply that Mr. Wishart did not want his horses to fall into the hands of anyone who might abuse them. Mr. Munroe in his testimony said that a similar provision directing that the horses be put to death was contained in an earlier will.
>
> At the Probate hearing Myles Wishart, one of the named Executors, said that Clive Wishart loved his horses and had purchased them to get them away from horse hauling matches and that he observed him feeding the horses sugar. Geraldine Christie, his sister, said that her brother Clive loved his horses and animals and when they would visit, he would take them to see his horses shortly after their arrival. She said his horses were treated "royally."
>
> Without question, Clive Wishart was always very concerned about the well-being of his four horses.

That said, Justice Riordan noted,

> Clive Wishart, just like any citizen has, had the right and privilege to make a will to bequeath and dispose of his property. Section 2 of the Wills Act R.S.N.B. (Royal Statutes of New Brunswick) 1973, chapter W-9.
>
> Why did Clive Wishart direct that his four horses be shot? In light of the fact that he held them in such high regard, and from what he told his solicitor Mr. Munroe, there can be no question that he did not want the horses to be abused if he was not able to provide for their welfare. There is, in my view, reason to believe that Clive Wishart would have wanted his horses to live if he had been aware that they would be attended to and properly cared for and not abused. The evidence is clear that he

> had a great love for his horses, and he was undoubtedly unaware that others would be prepared to provide and care for them and not abuse them. I, of course, have now the benefit of information that Clive Wishart did not have when he made his will. Many qualified persons are prepared to care for the horses.

He then addressed the issue of whether the execution of the four horses should be invalidated as against public policy. Usually, judges quote similar previous cases as relevant examples and guidelines. Riordan found no prior cases dealing with animals, so he resorted to referring to a collection of cases, mostly American, where deceased people had directed that their houses were to be demolished. In each case the house was perfectly sound and could have been sold to a new owner. Demolishing the houses would have reduced the estate's value, as vacant lots are an eyesore for neighbours. Each of the houses was saved from destruction by a court ruling.

> Should I be mistaken in my conclusion as to the real intention of Clive Wishart, legal authority is clear that, although the general rule is that the intention of a testator should be followed, it is not permitted to be performed where to carry it out would be contrary to public policy. In my opinion, the destruction of four healthy animals for no useful purpose should not be upheld and should not be approved. To destroy the horses would benefit no one and would be a waste of resources and estate assets even if carried out humanely. It is my conclusion that to destroy Barney, Bill, Jack, and King as directed in the will at this time and in the present circumstances would be contrary to public policy. The direction in the will is therefore void.
>
> In reaching this conclusion I in no way consider it to be a reflection upon Clive Wishart nor do I intend in any way to direct any criticism toward him. I think that he thought

> he was doing what he considered best for his horses. I do not think that when he prepared his will he anticipated that he would die only 14 months later.

The residuary (after payment of debts and taxes) beneficiaries named in Wishart's will were Verlin Wright and Victor Halberg of the state of Connecticut. Both said they had no interest in taking the horses. They agreed to give them to the Kings Landing Historical Settlement near Fredericton, an "outdoor living museum in which 19th Century New Brunswick comes to life" that "is comprised of approximately 300 acres and has over 70 period buildings, including homes, farms, a mill, a school, two churches, Kings Head Inn," according to its promotional material.

Many Tabusintac residents had grown to love the horses and had hoped they would stay in their community. "I hate to see them go. But if they have to go, they'll have to go and we'll have to say goodbye," said Lorne Harding, who had cared for the horses after Wishart's death and had fought for their survival.

"I guess we can go to Kings Landing, but it's not the same atmosphere," said Harding. "I don't think that's the kind of life Clive wanted for the horses. I think he'd want them up there running around the field like they are now.

"But I guess we can be thankful we saved their lives."

Postscript: About that touching letter from the "little Vancouver girl named Jennifer" to Justice Riordan begging him to save the horses, which he read aloud in court, Canadian Press news wire service discovered:

> A check of the address on the letter turned up no little girl named Jennifer.
>
> A woman who answered the telephone said her 49-year-old aunt is named Jennifer Buckland. She said Buckland is an animal lover but did not know who wrote the letter.
>
> Buckland, a flight attendant, was hiking in France and could not be reached.

A clerk at the court was surprised but a lawyer representing relatives of the late Clive Wishart, who owned the horses, said it makes no difference who wrote the letter.

"It doesn't take away from the fact that the whole country was concerned and that's all the judge was saying," said Dennis Lordon.

14

MCGILL UNIVERSITY WILL

The most important act of his life, James McGill wrote his will.

— CANADIAN NOVELIST HUGH MACLENNAN (1907–90)

MacLennan, who was an English professor at McGill University from 1951 to 1981, was referring to late eighteenth- through early nineteenth-century Montreal business magnate James McGill's pledge in his will to support the establishment of an institution of higher learning in Montreal to have the name "McGill." Some large donors give anonymously, not seeking credit; James wasn't of this ilk. He was one of the earliest, maybe *the* earliest, financial benefactors of a university to make such a demand.

One of Canada's wealthiest businessmen, James McGill died in 1813 at the age of sixty-nine. His will didn't provide an outright gift to establish the university; there were conditions. An ace at the art of the deal, James McGill regarded what he was doing as another deal in which he set the terms: My way or nothing. His strategy was "carrot and stick," a mixture of inducement and coercion.

His will promised that the province's Royal Institution for the Advancement of Learning would receive a large trust fund plus his forty-six-acre estate, "Burnside," at the foot of Montreal's Mount Royal, as the site for what would be the first university in Montreal, but only if a college bearing his name was built within ten years of his passing. If this condition wasn't met, everything would go to his stepson. The stepson, heavily in debt at the time of McGill's death, threw every legal obstacle possible to prevent the condition from being met so that he would get the money and land. Adding to the acrimony was that the will said the university was to be an English-language one, irritating the stepson, a French Canadian by birth. It was a microcosm of the disharmony between the English and French in Montreal and elsewhere in Quebec. Two distinct cultures — *Two Solitudes* as Hugh MacLennan titled one of his books — at odds and vying for supremacy.

Born in Glasgow, Scotland, on October 6, 1744, James McGill was the son of a prosperous merchant. After graduating from the University of Glasgow, he immigrated to Montreal in the late 1760s and went into the fur trade, then added general merchandise to his business, dealing throughout Lower Canada (Quebec), including with the Indigenous First Nations, and also with the northern United States, the West Indies, and Britain. He learned French to do business with French Canadians as well as English Canadians.

On December 2, 1776, James married Marie-Charlotte Guillemin Trottier Desrivières. Although Desrivières was Catholic, like the majority of French Canadians, the couple married in an Anglican service, James's religion. The daughter of a Montreal lawyer, Marie-Charlotte was the widowed mother of two boys, François-Amable and Thomas Hippolyte. James, who hadn't had children of his own, was reported to have treated his stepsons well.

Charlotte's excellent social connections quickly helped James move into Montreal's upper echelons, giving a boost to his business ventures. He served several terms as a justice of the peace and became a member of both the province's legislative assembly and executive council.

The family divided its time between a mansion James bought near Montreal's Notre-Dame cathedral, convenient for the Catholic-worshipping Charlotte, and Burnside. Since James had been born in Scotland, perhaps

Burnside was named in honour of Scottish poet Robbie Burns (1759–96), "the national poet of Scotland." The home was described as "large and commodious" by contemporary visitors. The estate wasn't a "gentleman's hobby farm," as only seventeen acres of the estate were cultivated, and that was in the form of gardens and an apple orchard.

James had more in common with stepson François, who shared his interest in business, than he did with Thomas, who instead was interested in military service. When old enough, François joined James's firm and was soon appointed a junior partner. Later, he was promoted to a senior partner. Thomas was killed in a duel in 1799, leaving behind a young son named James McGill "Guy" Trottier Desrivières. James took Guy into his home and paid for his upbringing and education.

McGill gave considerable thought to his will. He sought advice from John Strachan, a schoolmaster and ordained Anglican minister who was rector of Cornwall, Ontario, and from Scotland, like McGill. Their friendship dated back to when Strachan had come to Canada in the 1790s after a short time in the United States, and McGill had befriended the new arrival. Further linking them was that Strachan had married the widow of James's deceased brother Andrew, who'd also come to Canada from Scotland.

Strachan was an enthusiastic supporter of university education affiliated with religion. In 1827, he was instrumental in the establishment of King's College in Toronto, affiliated with the Anglican Church of England, and was its first president. He was also Toronto's first Anglican bishop. When King's College was secularized in 1848 and renamed the University of Toronto, Strachan, enraged that it no longer was religion-affiliated, started a privately operated Anglican-affiliated college nearby called Trinity College, which was federated with the U of T. (Trinity would later become open to students of all faiths.)

According to a record Strachan made of his conversation with McGill, he advised McGill: "Give by will some assistance for the future education of youth. It would be doing something to the glory of God and hand down your name with praise to posterity." McGill took up Strachan's idea of endowing in his will the establishment of a university, but he didn't accept Strachan's concept of affiliating it with religion. It was to be a secular institution.

The first half of McGill's nine-page will, drawn up with his lawyer on January 8, 1811, dealt with bequests to individuals; the second dealt with the university.

The first beneficiary named in the will was McGill's "dear wife" Marie-Charlotte. She received £2,000 outright plus a life annuity of £600, payable half-yearly. (Canada then used British currency.) François-Amable Desrivières inherited £23,000, extensive lands, and James's gold watch. Guy received £5,000 cash and another £5,000 to pay for his schooling. James also willed money and land to nineteen other people and five charities.

He then proceeded to his plan for a university. It was in two parts — first the land, then the money — both with the same four appointed administrators: Strachan; Montreal businessmen John Richardson and James Dunlop; and James Reid, a Montreal lawyer who would later become chief justice of Quebec from 1825 to 1848. All, like McGill, had emigrated from Scotland, had had great success, and were in the same upper society circle.

Instead of simply stating who was to get his land, he embarked on a mammoth 268-word, twenty-six-comma sentence with mind-numbing legalese, including "give and devise," "appurtenances," "convey," "hereinafter," "for uses, intents and purposes," and "intuited." Boiled down to its essence, it said that Burnside was to go the Royal Institution for the Advancement of Learning for the erection of a "University College." But it wasn't an outright gift; instead, McGill, ever a bargainer, said the institution had to build the college within ten years of his death and name it after him — a first-of-its-kind combined demand in a will.

The Royal Institution for the Advancement of Learning at all levels of schooling had been established by provincial legislation in 1801 but didn't get going until 1819.

The convoluted wording was as follows: "The said Royal Institution for the Advancement of Learning within the space of ten years to be accounted from the time of my decease do and shall cause to be erected and established upon the said tract or parcel of land a University or College for the purposes of education and the advancement of learning in the Province with a competent number of Professors and Teachers to render such establishment effectual and beneficial for the advancement of learning. The said College to be called McGill College." What a thicket of words!

This was followed by the instruction that, until a building was erected, his wife was to have "full use" of Burnside, and, on her death, this right would go to François-Amable. Further, if the university wasn't built by the ten-year deadline, there would be no extension but, rather, the property would go to François and his heirs.

Having dealt with the issue of land for a campus, McGill proceeded to the topic of money. He allocated £10,000 from his estate to be held in trust, as with the land, by John Richardson, James Reid, John Strachan, and James Dunlop, with the money to be paid, plus interest on it accrued from three years after his death, to the Royal Institution for the Advancement of Learning, provided that the university or college had been erected in his ten-year time frame. The will decreed: "It is to be applied towards defraying the expense in establishing the said University or College and towards maintaining it." The will went on to say again that if the ten-year date wasn't met, the money was to go to François or his heirs, the same as would happen with Burnside. (£10,000 in 1813 would be worth close to Can$1 million today.)

McGill died just under two years after writing his will, on December 19, 1813, from a short, unspecified to the public, illness. The *Montreal Gazette* wrote, "This venerable and respectable citizen had long and deservedly filled the most elevated stations in his community both as a magistrate and representative in the provincial Parliament for which his long residence, his fortune, and his talents eminently qualified him, and in the discharge of which he acquitted himself in a manner highly honourable to himself and useful to his country."

As it turned out, McGill's careful planning was for nought because he couldn't see into the future and didn't anticipate complications. As the saying goes, "The best-laid plans of mice and men often go awry," meaning that unforeseen events and circumstances can cause trouble.

James's grand plan began to unravel when his widow, Marie-Charlotte, died April 16, 1818, and per James's will, François received possession of Burnside in the interim until a college was built. There were five years to go until James's mandatory ten-year expiration date was to take effect.

Marie-Charlotte's death spurred action by both the Royal Institution and François that put them on a collision course. The institution, inactive since its inception, came to life, appointed a board, and began construction plans. For his part François did everything he could to prevent them.

His motive was simple: He was in desperate need of money. The wedding of his daughter Marie-Marguerite on January 13, 1818, and the dowry he gave her were costly. There were expenses associated with the many civic activities in which he participated, and with his and his wife Marguerite-Thérèse's elegant lifestyle.

François had also made what turned out to be an ill-timed choice to become an investor in and director of the Company of Proprietors of the Lachine Canal, which was to run through the southwestern part of the island of Montreal, making it possible to avoid the churning Lachine Rapids. Until the construction of the Lachine Canal, the rapids had to be portaged. For years Montreal merchants had sought the construction of a detour.

Unfortunately, getting the project going was a big headache, as problems kept cropping up. François's finances were badly hit. In August 1820, some of his property was seized for nonpayment of debt. He looked at the residuary clause of McGill's will as a lifeline, if only he could make the Royal Institution fail to meet the will's conditions. In late 1820, when the institution requested him to surrender Burnside, François refused, arguing that the institution had no funds with which to build a college and the government had given no undertaking that it would, so there was no reason he should move out.

More than money was at stake. The nature of the university itself was an issue. François was opposed to James's idea that it be non-denominational and that it be an English-language university; François, as his mother, Marie-Charlotte, had been, was French Canadian and a committed Roman Catholic. He was a churchwarden of Montreal's Notre-Dame cathedral and a friend of Quebec Roman Catholic Archbishop Joseph-Octave Plessis, who was opposed to the Royal Institution having a monopoly over education in the province, including of Roman Catholics.

Although François and his stepdad James McGill had got on harmoniously in business and socially, it's clear there was a great divide on cultural subjects. James's adviser had been the Protestant, English-language cleric John Strachan, while François's was the Catholic, French-speaking Plessis. François shared Plessis's view that the Royal Institution favoured the province's English population.

In response to François's refusal to relinquish Burnside, the Royal Institution launched two lawsuits against him, one to obtain Burnside and the other to receive the £10,000. Its position was strengthened when, in response to its application, it received a royal charter to found McGill College along with the authority to confer degrees. The institution contended that the charter meant the college was "erected" in law, in fulfillment of the requirements of McGill's will. François launched legal action against the contention, arguing that it contravened the wording of the will. To underscore his point, he hired as his senior counsel James Stuart, the lawyer who had drawn up McGill's will, implying that Stuart agreed with him.

The institution's title to Burnside was confirmed in 1822, one year before McGill's ten-year deadline expired. However, its victory was in principle, not actuality, because François ignored it and didn't budge from Burnside. In addition, he applied to Lower Canada's Court of Appeal for the decision to be overturned.

It was the equivalent of a chess match; one side made a move and the other a countermove, each seeking to block the other. In 1824 the institution appointed a principal, Archdeacon George Jehoshaphat Mountain, who'd earned plaudits for establishing public schools in Lower Canada providing free education to students who couldn't afford tuition at British-run private schools. François stayed put at Burnside.

In 1825 the Lower Canada Court of Appeal ruled against François. He appealed upward to the Privy Council in England, then the highest legal authority over Canada. Both he and the institution were laying out substantial money on legal fees. It took several years for the Privy Council to give a ruling, and during that time François continued to stay ensconced at Burnside.

Meanwhile, the university got a lucky break from an unexpected source — four medical doctors. The doctors, all from Edinburgh, yet another Scottish element in the story, were on staff at the new Montreal General Hospital, opened in 1820, and had established a medical teaching school in 1823 called the Montreal Medical Institution (MMI). But without a royal charter, the school couldn't grant degrees. It had students but no power to award degrees; McGill College had degree-granting powers but no students. The case for a merger was obvious, and discussions began in 1828.

While the talks were under way that year, the Privy Council ruled, as the previous courts had, in favour of the Royal Institution. François couldn't stall any longer. He finally gave in and vacated Burnside. McGill College and the Montreal Medical Institution merged in 1829, with the MMI becoming Canada's first faculty of medicine and simultaneously McGill's first faculty. The college at long last was operational. The Montreal General Hospital from which MMI had sprung became McGill's teaching hospital.

On June 24, 1829, when Burnside Place was formally opened as McGill College, there were still no classrooms on McGill's old estate — the first wouldn't come for another fourteen years — but teaching at McGill at last was a reality, sixteen years after McGill's death and six years after the "ten years from my death" he had stipulated.

There was still the matter of the £10,000 endowment. Not until 1835 did the Privy Council in Britain uphold the institution's claim to it. By that time, however, François-Amable Desrivières was no longer around; he'd died five years before.

15

THE ART GALLERY OF ONTARIO WILL

Toronto has always hated feeling second to its chief Canadian rival city, Montreal. This was how Toronto's art lovers were feeling at the beginning of the 1900s. Montreal had had a public art gallery, the Museum of Fine Arts, since 1879 and Toronto had nada. So embarrassing. The city's business, education, and political leaders along with artists, art teachers, and art appreciation clubs banded together and formed the Toronto Art Museum Association on March 15, 1900, with the goal of establishing a "Temple of Art" for the public. It got it by cajoling wealthy older Toronto couple Harriet and Goldwin Smith to agree to provide their spacious residence and its grounds, called "The Grange," for the site in their wills. It took ten years for the group's dream to become reality as Harriet died in 1909 and Goldwin the following year.

The Grange wasn't the Toronto Art Museum Association's first choice. At first it considered spots to the north — College Street at the head of McCaul Street and further north, at Bloor and Yonge. An owner of property in the Queen's Park area, west of Bloor and Yonge near the University of Toronto, said she'd sell it for $16,500 but wanted to keep use of it until 1908. Her proposal was rejected as being exorbitant, equivalent to $528,000 today.

The University of Toronto proposed that the group provide a $35,000 loan toward the construction of an addition to its Convocation Hall, in which there would be three main rooms to be used as exam halls with two also to be used for the display of artworks. This proposal went down with the association's members' council like a lead balloon, and the plan was abandoned.

As a makeshift solution until a site was found, artworks were exhibited from time to time at the city's Reference Library, then at College and St. George streets near the University of Toronto campus.

All these difficulties are why Edmund Walker, the head of the association, and also head of the Canadian Bank of Commerce (later CIBC), wanted The Grange.

The Grange was built in 1817 as the home of lawyer and merchant D'Arcy Boulton Jr., his wife, Sarah Ann, and their eight children. The Boultons and Sarah's family, the Robinsons, were prominent figures in the "Family Compact," a close-knit, wealthy, intermarried group that controlled all aspects of life in Upper Canada, as Ontario was then known. They were intertwined with the Protestant Orange Order lodges that controlled Toronto politics and the city's police force.

The Grange was located on one hundred acres that extended from Queen Street at the south to Bloor Street at the north, a distance of 3.3 miles, and from Beverley Street east to McCaul Street, 0.3 miles. It was a considerable distance from what was then central downtown Toronto. In its early days, before the growth of the city, bears roamed the grounds. On one occasion, the Boultons' pair of carriage horses struck at the bears with their fore hooves to drive them away.

The front door of the imposing mansion opened onto a central hall with the dining room on the left and the drawing room on the right. At the back of the house and on the second floor were bedrooms for the family. There were also four large rooms in the attic, probably for the servants. The kitchen, food storage areas, and scullery were in the basement. Originally, a path ran up to the front steps, flanked by an oval drive for carriages. The house was draped with ivy and stood on raised ground with terraces, as it does today. There was a glass-domed conservatory on the east side and a glassed orchard house for growing peaches, nectarines, and grapes. Around the residence was a mix of open spaces, stands of trees, and flower gardens. Behind the house were vegetable and fruit gardens and, farther north, an orchard. Other buildings included a stable, a root house, a tool house, and a drive shed where horse-drawn carriages were kept.

D'Arcy and Sarah Anne's eldest child was William Henry Boulton, born in 1812. He was a lawyer and prominent politician elected to the provincial legislature and served as mayor of Toronto for four terms. In 1846, when in Boston, he met beautiful, petite Harriet Dixon, thirteen years his junior, and the youngest child and only daughter of a wealthy Boston merchant.

William's father died on April 20, 1846, at age sixty. In his will, he bequeathed "all my real and personal property to my wife Sarah Ann Boulton." William and Harriet married November 16, 1846. They were painted in their wedding finery in separate portraits in oil on canvas by George Theodore Berthon, a leading portraitist of the rich and powerful in government and business. Harriet's showed her standing in her beautiful wedding gown; William was in a red velvet armchair with gold arms, knees crossed, wearing formal attire. Her picture, with the description "Portrait of Mrs. William Henry Boulton," hangs in the present-day Art Gallery of Ontario, and his, which the gallery also has, isn't on display.

William and Harriet lived at The Grange, secondary in rank to Sarah Ann.

In the 1840s and '50s, Harriet's money, or rather large infusions of money she had received over the years from her parents, was used to upgrade The Grange. The drawing room was expanded, the walls between three bedrooms on the second floor were knocked down to create space for a large assembly room, a wing was added as an office for William, the front hall was enlarged, and a new central staircase was installed with a painted glass window, still there, depicting the Boulton family crest — a hogshead (a large wooden barrel/cask that can hold sixty-three gallons of wine or sixty-four gallons of beer) pierced by an arrow. The family motto — *Dux vitae ratio* ("The guide to life is reason") — is below the crest.

There was a racecourse for a while, with a grandstand. There were nine servants; cottages were built on the grounds for married servant couples. A gatehouse was added in 1860, serving also as a home for William Chinn, an immigrant from London, England, whom William hired in 1858 to be his butler.

William and Harriet, whom he called "Hattie," held garden parties, picnics, sleigh rides, fancy dress balls, and tennis matches on the grass court on The Grange's front lawn. Haute Toronto attended, as did distinguished visitors to the city. Officers from the British Garrison in the city were invited too.

Harriet won prizes at fairs for her tatting, a type of lacemaking where the lace is fashioned from a series of tiny knots and loops of yarn or thread. Relatively easy to do, it was a popular technique in the 1800s, used for edging clothing and making doilies. Social columns in Toronto newspapers referred to her as "an excellent hostess." Grange-grown flowers were entered under William's name at flower shows and often won prizes.

Whenever Harriet's mother came for extended visits at The Grange, after Thomas Dixon's death in 1849, Sarah charged her $100 a month. For this sum Mary Dixon was to have the back dining room for a parlour and a bedroom, but Sarah took possession of the parlour, leaving Mary with just the bedroom, and still charged $100. "It should have been no more than $40 or $50 but my mother made no remarks," her son (Benjamin) Homer Dixon said.

The custom in that era was for a husband to have control over his wife's money, the rationale being that she didn't have the brains to handle it and that it was his right as head of the household. Harriet had been brought up in this tradition and on her marriage handed everything over to William, which was unfortunate because he was irresponsible, maladroit in business, and recklessly extravagant, and he piled up debts and increasingly overdrank. Harriet must have been close to saintly for putting up with him. Divorce was impossible in those days. For twenty years she paid the rent for his lease of the St. James Building, an office building in central downtown Toronto, and gave him money for repairs, which he never completed. William used his power of attorney over her business affairs to purchase stock in the Toronto, Grey and Bruce Railway, a bad idea because the line, which ran between two counties northwest of Toronto and Toronto, was beset by engineering problems and poor service and didn't last long. "A dead loss," Harriet's brother Homer said.

William double-crossed Homer in a real estate transaction and tried to mortgage parts of The Grange's property to his and his wife's relatives to pay off debts. Nobody wanted anything to do with the proposition.

Sarah Ann didn't want William to get The Grange when she died. To ensure that he didn't, she stipulated in her will: "I convey The Grange to the sole and separate use of my daughter-in-law Harriet Elizabeth Boulton free the debts or control of her husband of and during her natural life and immediately after her decease upon trust to and for such person or persons for such uses and such manner as said Harriet Elizabeth Boulton shall by will direct or appoint." The will left nothing — no property, no money, no personal possessions — to William.

Sarah Ann died August 1, 1863. Harriet now owned The Grange.

William died February 1, 1874, at age sixty-one. His death certificate stated "gentleman" as his "rank or profession." It gave as his "cause of death": "chronic disease of the brain." Alcoholism, also known as alcohol addiction, is described by medical texts as "a chronic disease of the brain. Over time, drinking too much alcohol can cause brain cells to die and a person's brain tissue to shrink."

Harriet was forty-nine when William died. Generally speaking, social conventions of the time dictated that while widowers could remarry after a few weeks, widows were expected to wait for a period from one to two-and-a-half years. Twenty months after William's death, on September 30, 1875, Harriet married Goldwin Smith, then fifty, a well-known writer and historian who had moved from England to the United States, then to Canada in 1871. He was two years older than Harriet, had never before married, was childless, and was independently wealthy. The *Dictionary of Canadian Biography* summarizes him as "writer, journalist, and controversialist."

Born in 1823 near London, England, Goldwin Smith was the son of an affluent physician and railway promoter. In 1858, at the unusually young age of thirty-five for such an honour, he was appointed Regius professor of history, the most prestigious rank of professor in the United Kingdom and Ireland, at Oxford University. He resigned in 1866 to care for his father, who had suffered permanent injury in a railway accident. In the autumn of 1867, when Goldwin was briefly absent, his father killed himself. Possibly blaming himself for the tragedy, and now without an Oxford appointment, Goldwin decided to resettle in the United States. He accepted an invitation to be part of the initial faculty at Cornell University in upper New York state, which opened in 1868. He refused a salary and from his own funds provided substantial financial support to the fledgling university as the need arose. He had his library shipped from England to enrich the small collection the college had gathered in its first months and provided a fund for further library development.

He came to Toronto in 1871. The many essays, book reviews, and letters he produced were printed in two hundred different periodicals and collected into thirty-six books. He was against war, home rule in Ireland, British and American "imperialism," women having the right to vote, trade barriers, socialism, Jews, and the new rich. He was for a commercial union of Canada and the United States but not a political one.

Canadian culture commentator Robert Fulford wrote in a retrospective in the *Toronto Star*, January 22, 1972: "Goldwin Smith was the most prominent essayist and opinion-monger of his time in English-speaking Canada and saw no reason to hide his opinions or his views."

In Smith's later years he came to be regarded as a "grand old man." His birthdays were observed with obsequious editorials and feature stories throughout Canada, and he was called "Toronto's first citizen" and "the sage of the Grange."

Smith had an outsized ego; dinner guests never got a chance to speak as he monopolized the conversation, expounding his views on anything and everything including subjects about which he had scant or no knowledge.

Harriet agreed to Goldwin's wish to have The Grange's conservatory torn down and replaced with a huge library. He called it "my temple of peace." He only permitted Harriet, his secretary Thomas Arnold Haultain ("Tabby"), and butler William Chinn to enter his sanctum sanctorum. There was a huge overflow; a billiard table in the middle of the room was strewn with books and manuscripts. "He said that if a fire broke out in the conservatory which was attached to the house the fire could spread to the house and therefore it should be replaced with his library," Chinn said. A rather peculiar argument, it seems, because should a fire have broken out in the library, the conflagration would be even worse considering all the paper in the room.

Harriet and Goldwin liked art and had paintings in their home. These included a watercolour he commissioned in 1880 of the front exterior of The Grange and its front lawn from Toronto artist Henri Perré, a landscape artist and art teacher who did many landscapes of Toronto and its vicinity.

Edmund Walker of the museum association broached the idea of the Smiths willing the Grange as a home for the Art Museum of Toronto in 1902, speaking to Goldwin who then spoke to Harriet. They both assented.

By that time, Harriet was seventy-seven and Goldwin seventy-nine. The big concern of Walker and the rest of the Art Museum Association's governing council was if Goldwin predeceased Harriet, her many nephews and nieces would persuade her to alter her will to give permission for the sale of The Grange with the proceeds to go to them. Goldwin, also worried about this possibility, accepted the association's suggestion that he say in his will that if he died before Harriet, she should appoint the "Art Gallery" trustees of the property, and if she refused, money should be given by his estate to the trustees to "appropriate" it. The wording was finalized in June 1902. The association was confident Harriet's relatives wouldn't object because more money would be obtained this way than if the property was put on the open market.

For this to happen the Art Museum had to be formally incorporated as an institution, and for that to happen provincial legislative approval was necessary. The association's lawyer, Zebulon Lash, and Smith's lawyer, John Greer, got together on September 9, 1902, three months after the deal with Smith, and drafted a bill to incorporate the institution. Lash wrote a memo the next day to the association's head Edmund Walker: "The old gentleman [Goldwin Smith] is anxious to have the matter put in definite shape as soon as possible."

"As soon as possible" turned out to be April 1903. Lash wrote Walker on April 29, 1903: "I sent to the clerk of the legislature last week the Art Museum Bill which Dr. Smith has approved of with the addition of the proviso I suggested to overcome his objection to mortgaging the property. The proviso being that no property given to the Museum should be changed or mortgaged contrary to the terms of the gift."

The bill was passed by the legislature.

Clause 12 of the act dealt with "Taking lands." It said,

> The Association may from time to time enter upon the lands of any person or corporation and survey the same and set out and ascertain such parts thereof as it thinks necessary and pay for carrying out the purpose and buy.

Following enactment of the legislation, Harriet and Goldwin formally drew up their wills. Harriet's began:

> WHEREAS under the last Will and Testament of Sarah Ann Boulton bearing date the 27th day of April, One thousand eight hundred and fifty-two, certain real and personal estate were devised to my sole and separate use during my natural life and from and immediately after my decease upon trust to and for such person or persons and for such uses and estates in such manner as I should by Will direct or appoint. Now in exercise of the powers for this purpose given to me by the said Will of Sarah Ann Boulton.
>
> I HEREBY GIVE DEVISE AND BEQUEATH to my husband Goldwin Smith for the term of his natural life the said lands and premises known as "The Grange."
>
> FROM and after the death of my husband, by virtue of the said recited power [Sarah Ann's will] I GIVE DEVISE AND BEQUEATH my said residence and grounds to "The Art Museum of Toronto" and their successors in fee simple for the purpose of an Art Gallery and Art Museum and for the purposes of the said "The Art Museum of Toronto" as set out in their Act of Incorporation.
>
> I GIVE DEVISE AND BEQUEATH to my husband Goldwin Smith all the furniture, pictures and household effects whatsoever belonging to me and including the whole of the contents of my said residence "The Grange"

> Toronto, and the contents of the stables and outbuildings, to include all the furnishings of the said residence for his sole and only use and benefit during the term of his natural life.

The will then proceeded to give one portion each of the residue to a long list of nephews, nieces, and friends. There were no other philanthropic bequests.

Goldwin's will began with monetary bequests to various individuals, starting with $5,000 to "my excellent Secretary, Theodore Arnold Haultain," to whom he gave all his manuscripts and unpublished works before he died. He bequeathed cash to a downtown Toronto nursing "mission," a couple of churches, some friends, and "my Louis Quatorze clock in the dining room to my Solicitor, G. Larratt Smith."

Then he got to the museum, at the bottom of the third page of his will:

> I BEQUEATH to the Art Museum of Toronto all my pictures, portraits or engravings and statuary which belong to me in The Grange and also my scrap-book and autograph book and any books on Art which may be in my library, and for the purpose of confirming my wife's devise of The Grange property to them I hereby devise and bequeath to them upon the same conditions as the devise to them in my wife's will, all right title and interest I may have or may have acquired in any manner whatsoever to The Grange property as more particularly described in her will, and as occupied by me since the time of my marriage.

In a following section he bequeathed his library collection to the University of Toronto.

He left the residue of his estate to Cornell University "to be used by the Board of Trustees for the promotion especially of liberal studies, languages ancient and modern, literature, philosophy, history and political science for which provision has been made in the new Hall which bears my name and to the building of which my wife has contributed."

The Goldwin Smith Hall at Cornell University was built in 1904, another example of Harriet's generosity to her husband.

Harriet died on September 9, 1909, of complications from a cold caught while on a carriage ride. Goldwin had her interred at St. James Cemetery, the final resting place for many of Toronto's rich and powerful, in a "box tomb," a structure resembling a rectangular box placed over an in-ground burial. Each side of its sloped "roof" was for inscriptions, one now for her, the other to be for him. It was typical of Goldwin's big ego that his name would be in larger letters than hers.

On September 25 the gift of The Grange in Harriet's will was announced. *The Globe* titled its story "The Grange, a Gift to the People."

On December 18, John Greer requested Toronto real estate appraiser Melfort Boulton to assess The Grange. Boulton submitted his report on January 12, 1910:

> This is a beautiful property with very fine lawns and handsome trees and the Residence is very substantial, though the main part is quite old, having been built in the year 1817. The inside woodwork is mostly black walnut, the rooms and main halls are large and spacious and the whole property having been well kept up is in good repair.
>
> I consider The Grange to be of the value for residential purposes of $85,000.

This was 21.5 times more than the $4,000 cost of building the house in 1817. The Art Museum was getting a fantastic deal; it was theirs for free ($85,000 in 1910 is equivalent to more than $2.7 million today).

Five months after the appraisal, Goldwin Smith broke a hip in an accident. He died at home in his beloved library a few weeks later on June 7, 1910. The flag at City Hall and those in other parts of the city were lowered to half-mast to honour him.

The public surged into the grounds. On June 13, 1910, a week after Goldwin's passing, John Greer's law partner G. Larratt Smith wrote Edmund Walker that this was causing a problem. "The servants in The Grange tell me today that they are bothered a good deal with people coming in who think The Grange is now public property and I would be glad if you would make a statement at the first opportunity you get in this connection or if you prefer that I should do so, I will attend to the matter."

The result was that just eight days later the museum and the city announced that four acres of the south part of the property behind the residence would become a public park called Grange Park, with the Art Museum to continue owning the land and the city managing the park. When the Art Museum of Toronto later morphed into the Art Gallery of Ontario (AGO), the agreement continued and still exists today.

The Art Museum of Toronto council met for the first time at The Grange on March 22, 1912. According to the council's minute book entry of May 26, 1913, "The executors of Mrs. Smith's estate offered to sell the Museum a sofa which had been in the dining room during Mrs. Smith's time at a minimum price of $35 [$923 today]. The Curator was instructed to purchase it if he thought advisable."

The Art Museum of Toronto was formally opened June 5, 1913. Ontario's then–lieutenant governor Sir William Mortimer Clark and Toronto's then-mayor Horatio C. Hocken took part in the dedication ceremonies.

Over the years bigger facilities were built on the site to accommodate the exponential increase in the artworks collection, but The Grange remains, designated a national historic site on June 8, 1970. It also is protected by the Ontario Heritage Act as "being of cultural heritage value." The premises now house a lounge for subscribed members of the gallery, a café (for lunch and afternoon tea), and exhibit space.

In 2015 The Grange Community Association applied for the "ceremonial name Harriet Boulton Smith Way to be assigned to John Street between Queen Street West and Stephanie Street," along the southern boundary of Grange Park. It was approved, a much-deserved honour for the woman who helped Toronto achieve its goal of creating a public art gallery for everyone.

16

VALID OR NOT?

While it is legally okay to write a holographic will on an unconventional thing like toilet paper, a facial tissue, a paper napkin, cardboard, or an envelope, it is not okay to be unclear in the wording. This is a common mistake in holographic wills that leads to the question: Valid or not valid?

The Paper Napkin Will

In June 2015, Saskatchewan resident Philip Langan was at the McDonald's restaurant at 94 Broadway Street West in Yorkton, which he often frequented, when he began to experience chest pains. Believing that he was about to have a fatal heart attack, he grabbed a thin brown McDonald's paper napkin and wrote on it:

> Ron Langan
> Dennis Langan
> Sharon Langan
> Landry Langan
> Philip W. Langan
> Marann Langan (Gust) [The actual spelling of her name was Maryann; he left out the *y*.]

> Dallas Langan
> Split my property evenly,
> "Dad Philip Langan"

Langan didn't die that day at McDonald's; that happened five months later, in November 2015, aged eighty. His son Landry had passed away in August, but Langan didn't revise his paper napkin will afterward, nor had he ever prepared a formal will. He'd only done this unusual holographic will, which he'd given to daughter Sharon for safekeeping. After her father's death, Sharon gave the will to her older brother Ronald, and he passed it on to his attorney, Bernard Stephaniuk.

Maryann Langan Gust was the only child who expressed skepticism about the authenticity of the will. On January 3, 2018, Stephaniuk delivered the napkin to Maryann's lawyer for Maryann to inspect. Maryann was still unconvinced. More time passed with her continuing to express doubt but not taking any legal action. That came on March 14, 2019, three years and four months after her father's death. She submitted an affidavit that said, "My Father told me in November 2015 that he wouldn't leave a will because he wanted us kids to fight like he had to. I wasn't able to verify the handwriting." Although she'd read the napkin and saw that her father had used her married surname in addition to her maiden name, she said, "He failed to refer to me by my married name 'Gust' although I had been married for some time and commonly used the name Gust." However, she didn't object to the financial terms.

Eight months later, Ronald, Sharon, and Philip Jr. gave affidavits contradicting Maryann at Stephaniuk's office. They all said they'd never heard their father say he "had no will or that he simply wished that his children would have to fight like he did." Ronald said the handwriting was his father's.

Sharon said, "I wasn't at McDonald's when he started writing on the napkin, but I observed him signing his name after, when he gave the document to me and said, 'This is my will. I want you to keep this in case something happens.' All the handwriting on it is his."

Philip said, "I wasn't at the restaurant when my father created the document, but I was when my father gave the handwritten document to Sharon and heard him tell her, 'This is my will and I want you to keep this in case something happens to me.' He was fully aware of what he was doing. He said he'd left out Earl because Earl had passed." Earl Langan, another of Phil's children, had died in 2006 at the age of forty-two.

The issue went to Justice Donald H. Layh of the Court of Queen's Bench-Yorkton. The many responsibilities of the Court of Queen's (King's) Bench include jurisdiction over probate and administration of estate matters. Justice Layh's written opinion was released February 2, 2020.

Before saying whether the will was or wasn't valid, he criticized both Maryann and Ronald:

> The court notes that Maryann is in error stating that the purported will fails to describe her using her married name. The document quite clearly refers to her using both "Langan" and "Gust."
>
> Ronald simply states that he is able to identify his father's handwriting on the document. However, Ronald does not exhibit a sample of his father's handwriting nor an analysis by a handwriting expert.
>
> Ronald states that he is aware other people were present and observed his father writing the document. Ronald does not identify who such "other people" may have been. The court is left to wonder why Ronald would not have identified those persons if he knew who they were or, more importantly, why these persons did not provide affidavit evidence to the court.

That said, Layh declared: "The court is satisfied that the document is a valid will and may be admitted for probate."

Although Phil Sr. thought he was dying at McDonald's, his napkin will was not a conditional will because he did not write, "If I die today here...."

All the siblings, including Maryann, agreed that Landry's portion should go to his children and that Earl's children also should receive from the estate.

Whether they afterward went as a group to Phil's favourite McDonald's is unknown.

Will A, B, or C?

In April 1990, Regina, Saskatchewan, resident Audree Eileen Bunn created three wills. When she died a dispute arose over which to go by — A, B, or C, as the court referred to them. The first, document A, was a single sheet of paper in her handwriting dated April 28, 1990, but not signed, in which she gave instructions for her funeral and made several bequests. The second, document B, was a printed will form also dated April 28, 1990, which named an executor. It revoked all former wills (she had handwritten one on September 15, 1987) but contained no directions as to the disposition of her estate. She signed this document in the presence of two witnesses. The third, document C, was identical in content to B except she hadn't signed it. The three documents were placed together in an envelope labelled "The Last Will and Testament of Audree Eileen Bunn — Executor — Allan Philip Dailey."

Bunn died on June 15, 1990, at the age of seventy-three, six weeks and six days after doing her wills A, B, and C.

The issue arose as to which will to follow. Should it be B because she had signed it, a requirement for holographic wills to be accepted? Or, because both A and B were written on the same date and were in the same envelope, should document A also be accepted because they were part of the same package? Saskatchewan's Court of Appeal said the latter made sense. Document C didn't matter because it was the same as B in content.

This was a case in which what seems to have been a rush job to get a will done resulted in a lack of clarity that led to bewilderment.

Sticky Notes

Ivo Giovanni Dalla Lana of Edmonton, Alberta, died March 5, 2018, at the age of ninety-two, four days after writing on two four-by-six-inch sticky notes what he described as "changes to my earlier will." That will had been done in 1997, nineteen years earlier. Which should be accepted? It depended on the interpretation of his word "changes": Were the changes just tinkering or were they a complete redo?

Dalla Lana and his wife, Mary, had been married for sixty-one years at the time of his death. They had five sons — Gene, Eric, Tom, Steve, and John — and ten grandchildren.

Signed, dated, and written in block letters, the first of the two sticky notes said,

> Changes to my earlier will.
> ERIC'S SON [R] WAS LEFT MONEY, DELETE THIS PROVISION.
> GENE TO BE EXECUTOR
> TOM TO BE CAN'T REMEMBER TITLE BUT ONE STEP LOWER THAN EXECUTOR. (FORMS GUY)
> TWO PROPERTIES ARE TENANTS & COMMON

These instructions having filled the first sticky note, Dalla Lana continued on the second sticky note:

> THESE PROPERTIES TFR TO MARY AUTOMATICALLY.
> TFSA TO TOM
> PORTFOLIO RESULTS. 20K TO EACH SON
> 10K TO EACH OF 10 GRANDCHILDREN
> REST OF ESTATE GOES TO MARY.
> CONVERT USD TO CHECKING ACCOUNT.
> PAY BILLS BY DISBURSEMENTS.

The issue was sorted out by Alberta's Court of Queen's Bench. It unequivocally said the sticky notes should prevail. "The Court finds the notes to be thorough in nature as they address all his estate."

Importance of Signing

A signature takes only a moment to write. Despite the decline of handwriting in this digital age, a handwritten signature still is required under the law for wills.

Not providing a signature on a will can lead to a tug of war over an estate. A case in point is *Langseth Estate v. Gardiner*, a dispute that went to Manitoba's Court of Appeal on the death of Melvin Ernest Langseth of Neepawa, a small community in northwest Manitoba, who died October 22, 1988, at the age of sixty-seven. He was a widower with no children.

The Court of Appeal justice presiding over the case was Sterling Rufus Lyon, on the court since 1986, previously having served as Manitoba's premier. Representing the estate were Melvin's co-executors, his sister, Sylvia McKie, and brother, Russell Arthur Langseth, who under Melvin's will were to receive the residue of the estate after specified bequests were made. On the other side was Viola Ada Gardiner, one of the specified beneficiaries who was to receive … and here was the nub of the quarrel. Sylvia and Russell thought it should be $3,000 as Melvin had stated in a typewritten will done in 1973 and signed in full. Viola thought it should be the $20,000 Melvin wrote in a handwritten memorandum to his will in 1988. This memorandum wasn't dated nor signed in full but was initialled. Sylvia and Russell said initialling didn't meet Manitoba's wills regulation calling for a full signature in ink; Viola contended that the initialling was enough.

The exact nature of Viola's relationship to Melvin is unclear. She said, "I started keeping company with him in 1962 and lived with him in his Neepawa residence as man and wife from 1972 until his death October 27, 1988." To which Justice Lyon said:

> I deal first with a small point that is not germane to the case. I am not satisfied that Ms. Gardiner was a "common-law wife" of the deceased. The testator expressly said she was his housekeeper and not his common-law wife. I would not want to contradict the deceased without more than her assertion of a state of affairs contrary to his formal statement. However, I do not think this concern has anything to do with the issues before us.

Viola further said, "I was the principal breadwinner until 1987 when I quit to take care of him because he was then in ill health." She worked at

Neepawa's Osborne Home for Senior Citizens, a retirement home, from 1972 to 1974, then at East View Lodge, a seniors' long-term care facility in Neepawa, until 1987.

In a will he wrote April 10, 1973, Melvin included a bequest of $3,000 "to my friend, Viola Ada Gardiner." Soon after he scratched out $3,000 and replaced it in handwriting with $5,000. That change was carried forward into a new will of June 17, 1975, in which the bequest to Viola read, "The sum of Five Thousand Dollars ($5,000.00) to my friend, Viola Ada Gardiner." Sometime later — the exact date wasn't given — he wrote a memorandum upping the sum to $20,000. He initialled it rather than signing it in full, and he didn't date it. On October 12, 1988, which would turn out to be two weeks before his death, he wrote, "I, Melvin Ernest Langseth, being of sound mind do declare that Viola Ada Gardiner is my housekeeper and not my common-law wife." Why he felt it important to make this statement is unknown.

Melvin had also stipulated that Viola was "to get my cars: '65 Buick, '79 Oldsmobile, '66 Ford, and '71 Ford half-ton truck." These weren't part of the court case.

What stood out was that the other specified bequests totalled $6,300 compared to Viola's $20,000. Nieces and nephews were to get a total of $6,000, and a woman who "took care of my father while he was in hospital" was allocated $300.

On November 7, 1990, Justice Lyon ruled that the initialling was sufficient: "The alteration was initialled by the deceased and courts have long accepted initials as sufficient to meet the formal requirement of signing." Viola received the full $20,000. She lived for twenty-seven more years, dying in 2017, three weeks short of what would have been her ninety-second birthday. Her obituary started by saying that she was predeceased by her parents, four brothers, a sister, and "special friend Melvin Langseth."

Valid

On September 16, 2018, Nicola Maria Cordani, a middle-aged British Columbia woman with a long history of bouts of depression and anxiety, was found dead by police on the bank of the province's Fraser River near New Westminster, part of the Greater Vancouver Area. Her car was parked nearby. In it the police found a handwritten note she'd left on the driver's seat. The note was a suicide message interposed with a will. The will named Jean-Claude Gregoire, "common law husband," the chief beneficiary. Instances of a will being contained in a suicide note are rare.

Nicola and Jean-Claude met in 1999 while they were both employed at Canada Post. They became romantically involved in 2000. The affair ended in 2009 due to her challenges with anxiety and depression. They continued to be friends. In April 2015, Nicola attempted to take her life and was hospitalized. She reached out to Jean-Claude, and he visited her every other day. She told him she had previously attempted to take her life in 2013 and that she needed someone to help her. After a month-long hospitalization, Nicola was discharged, and Jean-Claude visited her once or twice a week. He then changed his shift at work so he could be with her more. For most of 2015 he visited Nicola every other day.

As of early 2016 Jean-Claude was staying full-time at Nicola's apartment. Nicola commenced a gradual return to work but suffered a relapse of anxiety and went on disability. Later that year, they agreed he should move into her apartment permanently. Jean-Claude kept his own rental apartment until the end of the year, mainly for storage as her apartment was short on space.

In the early fall of 2017, she told Jean-Claude she was going to "cut out" her mother, Catherina, and two of her brothers, Steven and Adam, from her life. She stopped communicating with them. She told Jean-Claude she felt they "haven't supported me in the way I need." She remained close with a third brother, Michael.

According to Jean-Claude in February 2018, Nicola became manic and delusional. With Michael's assistance, he had her admitted to hospital for two weeks. Following her stay, she seemed improved. After this hospitalization the couple discussed executing wills and designating each other as the beneficiary of their Canada Post pensions, but they didn't proceed. In May 2018, Nicola reached the limit of her disability leave and it was possible her employment would be terminated unless she returned to work. She returned and was able to work up to thirty hours per week.

On September 13, 2018, when Jean-Claude returned home from work, Nicola wasn't there. He'd last seen her at 6:45 a.m. when he went to work.

He filed a missing person's report with the New Westminster Police on September 15. The following day the police found her body and the suicide note and will.

They told Jean-Claude it wasn't permissible for them to release Nicola's suicide note/will itself, but they provided him with a certified copy.

The will portion said Jean-Claude, "common law husband," was to receive her apartment and all its contents plus the money in two bank accounts she had. Her brother Michael was to get her registered retirement savings plan (RRSP) money. She wrote about her two other brothers: "Steven + Adam Cordani get nothing."

There could have been a problem over Nicola leaving her RRSP to her brother Michael because when she'd got the RRSP, she'd made her mother Catherina the beneficiary and had never changed this even after she and her mother became estranged. However, Catherina raised no objections to Michael getting it. The will was declared valid.

Not Valid

Joseph Philip Joy ("Jody"), of Barrie, Ontario, took his own life on July 13, 2019, at the age of forty-seven, leaving a suicide note with a will that was the complete opposite of one he'd done in 2016, leading to a court battle over which should prevail.

The 2016 will left bequests to Jody's stepson, Michael McGrath (from his first marriage to Jacqueline McGrath); Michael's son, Michael Jr.; Jody's second wife, Joanne; and Dexter Ramsundarsingh, Jody's long-time friend and a shareholder in his electrical business. Dexter was to receive Jody's interest in the electrical business. Joanne Joy, whom Jody met in 2013 and married in 2016, was to receive the after-tax proceeds of a $600,000 life insurance policy.

In his suicide note, Jody expressed an intention to void Joanne's interest in his estate, made no mention of Dexter, and left substantial additional benefits to Michael and Michael Jr.

Joanne and Dexter went to Ontario Superior Court, which has jurisdiction over wills, to get the note declared invalid on the grounds that Jody had lacked "testamentary capacity" because he had a history of substance abuse and committed suicide after a full day of drinking and smoking hash oil cigarettes, "which is clear from the sloppy and all over the place handwriting, many spelling errors, and words crossed out." The note also included a profane diatribe against Joanne.

Stepson Michael wanted the suicide note to supplant the 2016 note as he and his son stood to receive more under the suicide note will.

The court gave its decision on December 2, 2020. It agreed with Joanne and Dexter that the suicide note should be declared invalid, giving its reasons as follows: "The handwritten note was sloppy and nearly illegible. Jody was depressed, according to his sister. The excessive use of alcohol and hash oil cigarettes was a part of his daily life according to those who knew him best."

Friendship or Undue Influence?

Did eighty-one-year-old Clarence Hay leave the bulk of his $320,000 estate to a twenty-seven-year-old woman he'd known for a short time and make her the executrix rather than his immediate family because of friendship or undue influence? She said it was friendship; his relatives alleged the will was prepared "under suspicious circumstances — undue influence" by her and she shouldn't get anything.

Hay never married and was childless. He lived alone on his farm near Belleville, Ontario, which he actively farmed in an old-fashioned manner with horses. On July 11, 1985, he wrote his will, leaving one of his two farms and most of the rest of his estate to Sandra Florence Vout, a young woman in her twenties. Vout, a denture therapist, and her mother were frequent visitors to the Hay farm, helping him bale hay, clean barns and stalls, shovel manure, and water and feed his horses. "We were good friends," she later said. "I really enjoyed his company. He was a very, very good man." There were never allegations of a sexual relationship between the two.

Also in the will Hay bequeathed his other farm to a nephew, $1,000 to his brother Carl, and $3,000 each to his seven nephews and nieces. This was his second will. He'd done one twenty-two years earlier, on April 26, 1966, in which he left an equal amount to his brother, Earl, and his sister, Florence, who died in 1970.

Hay's farm wasn't near others. He was isolated. On June 28, 1988, relatives who went to check on him found him dead. His body was severely bruised, making it evident that he'd been badly beaten — murdered. When police learned of the new will, Vout became a suspect in Hay's killing. They interviewed her on July 6, 1988, and cleared her. On September 11, an Oshawa, Ontario, man was charged with the murder. He confessed that he was a drug addict and had attacked Hay with an iron bar and a piece of wood in an attempt to get money for drugs. He pleaded guilty at trial and was sentenced to life imprisonment. "This was a vicious, cowardly attack," the presiding judge, Ontario Supreme Court Justice W.D. Chilcott, said.

Hay's relatives were stunned to learn that he had drawn a second will that largely left them out in favour of Vout. They said they had been in close contact with him but had a general lack of knowledge of a relationship between Vout and him. Unhappy with the will, the relatives challenged it, arguing that there were "suspicious circumstances" about it. "Suspicious circumstances" can be that the will-writer lacked the mental "testamentary" capacity to write a will or was subject to "undue influence" — in other words, coercion.

The first court to hear the case was the Ontario Superior Court, Justice Richard Byers presiding, in 1990.

The evidence revealed that the will was prepared by a legal secretary in the office of Vout's parents' lawyer. One secretary drew the will, and she and another secretary witnessed its execution. It was a one-lawyer firm, he wasn't involved in the preparation and execution of the will, and no record or file was kept. The secretaries gave evidence only from their memory of the execution of the will, and their evidence differed as to where in the lawyer's premises — the waiting room or an office — the will was signed.

The secretary who prepared the will, Lois Clark, testified on cross-examination that she had received her instructions from a woman who identified herself as Vout. The woman telephoned several times, but the witness did not recall whether the instructions were received by telephone or by an attendance at the office. When Vout and Hay came to the law office, Clark recognized Vout's voice as the voice on the telephone. Clark testified that she read the will to Hay in the waiting room in front of Vout.

On cross-examination, Clark stated that Hay at some point during the reading of the will "hesitated" and "had a quizzical look on his face." When questioned about what happened next, the secretary said, "He looked at me, and I looked at him, and up at Sandra, he looked at Sandra and she stated, 'Yes, that's what we discussed. That's what you decided,' and he nodded to go on, to continue."

The two secretaries witnessed the will and Vout paid the bill. In Canada, almost anyone can be a witness to a will, including the person who prepares the will and the executor. The only people who aren't allowed are a beneficiary, the person's spouse, or anyone else who has a vested interest in the will. They must also be of legal age (eighteen or older) and mentally capable at the time of signing.

When Sandra Vout was asked why the deceased would leave so much of his estate to her, she replied, "I suppose it was because he was fond of me."

Justice Byers ruled that the will was valid and therefore qualified for probate, saying that "Mr. Hay was old and eccentric, but alert, smart, independent, determined, and most important, not easily influenced. He had capacity and was not unduly influenced. The hard reality is that the Hay family simply cannot accept that Clarence Hay might really have intended to leave a large portion of his estate to someone outside of the family, nor can they comprehend why he might want to do that."

The relatives continued to believe that there'd been "suspicious circumstances," referring to the law firm being selected by Vout and her participation when the law secretary went over the will. They appealed to the Ontario Court of Appeal "to set aside" Justice Byers's decision. It agreed in 1993, scolding Byers in their decision. "In our respectful opinion he erred in basing his decision entirely on the mental competence of the deceased. He failed to consider properly the equally important issue of whether there had been suspicious circumstances surrounding the execution of the will."

Vout appealed to the Supreme Court of Canada. Its unanimous decision was delivered on June 22, 1995, by Justice John Sopinka, seven years after Hay's demise. The court sided with Vout, declaring that in its opinion she hadn't exercised undue influence or coercion. Sopinka wrote, "I am satisfied that the trial judge scrutinized the evidence to the degree required. He obviously was of the view that this fully competent, self-reliant and independent-minded individual would not have made the will as he did if he had not appreciated fully what he was doing."

17

THE CEMETERY WILL

What happens if an organization named as the trustee of a bequest in a will goes out of existence? Does it mean that the money can no longer be used for the beneficial purpose intended?

That was the unusual situation that arose from a clause in a will that set up a trust fund for maintenance of a historic cemetery in the Niagara, Ontario, region. The author of the will was George Franklin Tufford, a member of a long-time prominent southern Ontario family who died October 28, 1967, at age ninety-eight.

In his will, Tufford wrote:

> All the rest and residue of my estate shall be invested by my executors until the death of my said sister at which time, after payment of legacies, the remainder of my estate shall be converted into cash and the net balance is to be paid by them to the trustees of the Mennonite Cemetery at Campden, Ontario. Such balance shall be invested, and the interest thereon be used for the upkeep of the said Cemetery.

The sister died in 1981, aged 103 years. The estate was valued at that time in excess of $250,000 ($843,815 today).

Tufford wasn't a Mennonite. He and his wife, Mary, who predeceased him, weren't interred at the cemetery but at one in a nearby township. His parents also weren't Mennonites. However, his paternal grandparents and his paternal great uncle had been and were interred at the cemetery.

The cemetery, full name Mennonite Mountain Cemetery, is of heritage significance, a historic link to the Mennonites' early settler days in the British colony of Upper Canada (now Ontario). Many Mennonites living in Pennsylvania chose to depart after the United States became independent in the American Revolutionary War (1775–1783) and accepted the offer of the British colonial government of inexpensive land in Ontario's Niagara Escarpment region. The first arrivals included forebears of George Franklin Tufford.

The Mennonites' occupation was farming, and the escarpment has ideal soil for growing what are called "tender fruits" — peaches, pears, plums, grapes, cherries. Many of the Niagara Escarpment Mennonites, including the Tuffords, settled in Lincoln County in the west. They erected wood-frame "meeting-houses" where they worshipped.

One of their farming communities in Clinton Township in Lincoln County was Campden. In 1843 David Moyer, a member of the community, in a "deed of gift," gave a half acre from the northeast corner of his farm for a "church," Campden Mennonite Church, and cemetery, Campden Mennonite Cemetery.

Early in the 1900s, Campden Mennonite Church congregation merged with the congregation of the First Mennonite Church of nearby Vineland. Campden's "church" closed in 1908, but the cemetery continued to be used as a burial place. So far, the Niagara Peninsula branch of the Ontario Genealogical Society has recorded inscriptions of 258 faded gravestones, among them a number bearing the surname "Michener," part of the family tree of Roland Michener, Canada's governor general from 1967 to 1974. There are numerous people surnamed "Tufford" also interred at the cemetery. It's a treasure trove of information about the past for genealogists and historians.

The merged congregation established a board of trustees, and a separate bank account was kept for the maintenance of the cemetery. The last cemetery board was appointed for a one-year term in 1942. Thereafter the general board of trustees of the First Mennonite Church at Vineland maintained the cemetery and kept the trust fund.

In 1965 the council of the Township of Clinton passed a bylaw to acquire the cemetery and assumed responsibility for it in 1966. The trustees of the First Mennonite Church at Vineland began to transfer the cemetery trust funds to the township. All this happened before Tufford's death in 1967.

Tufford didn't change his will to reflect the change in administration. At his death it still said the money was to go to the Trustees of the Mountain Mennonite Cemetery Campden for maintenance of the cemetery. This created a legal problem as that entity no longer existed. Did this mean that Tufford's money could never be used for the beneficial purpose he'd intended?

In 1974 the Town of Lincoln (the successor of the Township of Clinton) enacted a bylaw by which it assumed responsibility for thirteen "abandoned" cemeteries located throughout the municipality, including the Mennonite Mountain Cemetery.

The Town of Lincoln sought direction from Ontario's Superior Court as to whether it could receive the money as the present administrator.

Ontario Superior Court Justice James Southey declared that the money was a specific benefit and therefore couldn't be rerouted. He said, "The Trustees of the Mennonite Cemetery at Campden, Ontario, no longer existed at the date of the death of the testator and because that cemetery was no longer being cared for by any Mennonite organization, there was a lapse or failure of the residuary bequest to those trustees and the residue must now be distributed as an intestacy."

When an intestacy is declared, the money usually goes to next of kin, which meant that relatives of Tufford would benefit. They were willing for a sufficient portion to go to the Town of Lincoln for the cemetery's upkeep and joined the town in asking the Ontario Court of Appeal to allow this. "Many years ago, he expressed concern over the neglected condition of the cemetery, and he erected a memorial there to his grandparents and uncle,"

Muriel Tufford, a niece, said in an affidavit filed with the court, expressing the view of the family. "I do not believe he intended to benefit the Mennonite Church generally or Mennonite cemeteries generally. Rather, I believe he intended only to preserve this particular cemetery so as to protect the graves and memorials of his relatives."

Writing for the court, Justice Francis Stephen Weatherston said in February 1984:

> Where a testator leaves the residue of his estate to the trustees of a cemetery operated by a church, but control over the cemetery has passed to the municipality before the testator's death, the gift does not lapse if the testator intended to benefit not the particular charity but rather the particular charitable purpose. In those circumstances the trustees to whom the bequest is made are merely the channel for carrying out the purpose.
>
> It is apparent that George Tufford intended the gift to be applied for the upkeep of the cemetery and the gift should be allowed to take effect by appointing the municipality as the new trustee.

That said, Weatherston provided "direction":

> In my opinion, therefore, the gift here in question was a valid charitable bequest notwithstanding the demise of the trustees. A new trustee should be appointed, the most obvious one being the Corporation of the Town of Lincoln, there being no cemetery board. The bequest is to be held in trust in a separate account for the maintenance of the named cemetery.

As for the relatives' request for "surplus money" to go to them, Weatherston said no. "Since the trust was 'forever' the need likely will arise to dip into any surplus as time passes." He elaborated:

> It is apparent that the phrase a "general charitable intention" is used in different senses in different contexts. It is sufficient in this case to say that the will discloses an intention that the residue to the estate is to be used for a particular charitable purpose which is capable of being performed, but that the testator made an error as to the amount of money required to accomplish that purpose, probably because his sister lived so long. There was nevertheless an intention to dedicate the entire residue to charity forever, and so there can be no resulting trust in favour of the next of kin.

He wound up:

> The order of Justice Southey should be set aside and in place thereof there should be an order that the residuary bequest passes to the Corporation of the Town of Lincoln in trust for the upkeep of the Mennonite Cemetery at Campden, Ontario. If and when it is found that there is more than sufficient income for that purpose, the Town of Lincoln is to be at liberty to propound a scheme for the administration of the surplus money.

This isn't the end of the story. More followed.

In 2009 local historian Larry Rittenhouse reported to police what he initially thought was vandalism — grave headstones had been "snapped off and broken" at the cemetery. In a second call, this time to the Town of Lincoln, he was told that staff had directed its maintenance workers at the cemetery to lay down stones that could be a possible hazard because of their deteriorated condition. Next, he contacted reporter Joanne McDonald of the local newspaper *Niagara This Week*. She interviewed him and her story was published on page one on October 6, 2009.

Rittenhouse told McDonald,

> They didn't do this in bad faith, but they've hurt a lot of people and destroyed many stones. They did what they thought was right, but it was wrong. I counted 24 stones broken on the ground plus two leaning and five pushed off their base with the holding pins exposed. I found one stone behind a large tree, another three large stones inside overgrown bushes, and under another bush many fragments and pieces of stone.
>
> These are the very earliest pioneer settlers of the Campden area and their descendants. These were the people who built this community and left it as a gift to us.
>
> The area around each stone should be dug out and the stones laid on a slope on a bed of gravel to prevent further deterioration.

McDonald also interviewed Lincoln Chief Administrator Officer Anne Louise Heron. She said, "Parks and facilities staff were directed as part of normal procedure to carry out the work of laying down stones. Regular upkeep includes cutting the grass and where there are broken stones, you lay them so the stone is laying from head to foot on the grave." This statement, though, doesn't explain the cavalier treatment of the stones as described by Rittenhouse.

Sandra Easton, a grand-niece of George Tufford, wanted the Town of Lincoln to spend some of the differential between the maintenance costs and the interest made on the trust to repair the damage done by the workers. The accumulated interest by year-end 2008 was $196,143 for a total trust value of $462,110. During 2008 the interest earned was $21,056 and maintenance costs $6,325.

"Whoever laid down the stone of my great-great-grandfather Manasseh Tufford created additional damage that is evident by two additional chunks of the stone and confirmed by bright, white broken edges," Easton said.

Heron rejected Easton's suggestion, saying, "Reconstruction is different from upkeep, which includes cutting the grass and ensuring that safety measures, such as gates, fences and trees are kept in proper order. The

Town, however, doesn't own the monuments and cannot undertake works to privately-owned markers."

Easton, however, wasn't satisfied. A few years later, she was elected mayor of the Town of Lincoln, and on May 1, 2017, she spearheaded the passage of a bylaw declaring the cemetery to be a "heritage property" under section 29 of the Ontario Heritage Act 1990 because of its "cultural value and interest." Section 29, "designation of individual properties," empowers a municipality with the legal authority and jurisdiction to determine if a heritage property will be preserved.

Designation as a heritage property prohibits the demolition or removal of any building or structure and requires approval by the provincial government's heritage minister for alterations to the property. The goal "is to manage change on heritage properties to ensure they retain the historic characteristics that make them special." Designation also makes property owners eligible for preservation grants and tax relief.

George Franklin Tufford, your will did what you wanted. You can rest in peace.

18

LOCK BOX

Which of two wills found in Eleena Violette Murray's lock box at her Kitsilano, British Columbia, home should prevail? This case featured a tangled story of fuzzy memories, contradictory evidence, some outright lies, quirkiness, and the impact of aging, relevant to many Canadian families, as an object lesson. At stake was an estate worth $1.4 million.

Eleena, a childless widow, died October 4, 2017, at age ninety-nine and a half, in the midst of planning a celebration for her one hundredth birthday, a process she'd begun when she was ninety-six. She left behind two wills in her lock box in her home. A formal signed, notarized, dated will done in 2013 made the British Columbia Society for the Prevention of Cruelty to Animals (BCSPCA) a major beneficiary and her relatives minor ones. Another will was done in 2017, the year of her death. It was unsigned, undated, unnotarized, stroked through, and said the exact opposite: The relatives should be the major beneficiaries and the BCSPCA the lesser.

If the later unsigned "note" prevailed over the earlier signed will, Eleena would be declared to have died "intestate" — without a will. When this happens, the court decides where the money should go and next of kin get priority. Under this scenario, relatives stood to receive a lot of money because the specific gifts named in the note didn't absorb much of the estate.

In their submissions to British Columbia's Supreme Court, the plaintiffs, the group wanting the note to be accepted, described it as a codicil to the 2013 will altering some of its terms, not an entirely new will. The onus was on them to prove that Eleena had testamentary capacity and knowledge and approval of the content of the note. The BCSPCA argued that Eleena lacked the requisite "testamentary capacity" to execute the note or revoke her 2013 will. Because testamentary capacity is a matter of legal interpretation, opinions of doctors aren't regarded as essential or conclusive. It's recognized that, particularly with the elderly, cognition is "amorphous and seldom static."

In her August 20, 2021, decision, BC Supreme Court Justice Heather MacNaughton described Eleena as a

> senior who was clearly remarkable for her age. She was a character loved by friends and family despite having strong opinions, being bossy, and knowing her own mind. She loved the theatre and the arts and enjoyed dressing up. Her birthdays were important celebrations and she was looking forward to those for her 100th birthday.
>
> Ms. Murray loved animals, wild and domesticated. She was a dog owner and welcomed her friends' dogs into her home. She never drove; she walked or took the bus to meet most of her needs. For many years, and well into her nineties, she walked from her home to the duck pond at Jericho Beach to feed the birds, particularly the ducks, and the rabbits and squirrels. A round trip took her between one and a half hours to two hours.
>
> After she moved into a long-term care facility, where she spent the last months of her life, Ms. Murray visited a horse that lived behind the home and fed it carrots. She asked her nephew Brian to buy a salt block for it.

MacNaughton added, "Ms. Murray was fiercely independent and was not someone to tangle with. She was not afraid to disagree with people and was described as feisty. She made friends and kept them, but she could be unforgiving if someone crossed her."

Eleena, called "Lynn" by family and friends, lived in her own home at 2327 Collingwood Street in Kitsilano until March 2017, when she was hospitalized for ill health, then transferred to a long-term care home. Developed as a less expensive suburban alternative to Vancouver's West End district, Kitsilano's proximity to downtown Vancouver, numerous parks, and big Kitsilano "Kits" Beach make it a desirable place to live. With their gabled roofs and broad verandas, well-preserved homes on Collingwood Street were appreciating in value, which would make Eleena's house a focal point in the conflict.

Eleena's first will was prepared on November 5, 2010, by Vancouver area lawyer Gerrit J. Te Hennepe. After providing for payment of the estate's debts, expenses, taxes, and probate fees, the will divided the residue of the estate into fourteen equal parts, with shares going to nephew Ron Tekano, grand-nephew Tim Henderson, niece Verna Hancock, Verna's daughters Gina Hancock Bernier and Carla Hancock Leversage, and the BCSPCA. The other beneficiaries were extended family members of her deceased husband.

On January 25, 2013, Eleena revoked the 2010 will and did a new one, which was notarized by Kitsilano notary public Hilde Deprez. This will appointed Eleena's friends Joyce Myler, whom she'd known for sixty years and who was about twenty years younger, and Elizabeth Jones as co-executrices. It allotted $60,000 each to her niece Verna Hancock, her grand-nieces Gina and Carla, and her grand-nephew Tim Henderson. It left $40,000 each to nephews Ron Tekano and Daniel Henderson, her deceased husband's brother, Don Murray, and two of his nieces, Constance Kennedy and Julia Hawks, and the residue to the BCSPCA.

According to Tim Henderson, to whom the 2013 will left money, and his father, Brian, not named a beneficiary but whose brother, Daniel, had been, Eleena's health began to decline in late November and December 2016.

In addition to being Eleena's nephews, Daniel and Brian were her godsons. Brian lived in the Kootenay mountain region in southeastern British Columbia, 520 miles east of Vancouver. He testified that "in about

November and December 2016, she told me things on the phone and I didn't understand what she was talking about. She was confused about which aisle she had left her shopping cart at the grocery store. She'd left a pot burning on the stove."

Tim was a clinical nurse educator at Vancouver General Hospital. He said that in mid-December 2016, concerned that she wasn't answering her phone, he went to check on her:

> I found her on the kitchen floor, delirious. I had her taken to VGH [Vancouver General Hospital] where I was told that she'd suffered a stroke and had a urinary tract infection.
>
> She was at VGH from December 17–28. When she was released, she was close to her normal self. She was weak physically but had improved from when she was admitted. I took the last part of December off work and moved into her Collingwood home to care for her. When I returned to work in January 2017, I continued to reside in the Collingwood home. My father [Brian] moved from the Kootenays into the home to care for her when I was at work.

Brian said,

> When I arrived, I found cheques she hadn't cashed and bills she hadn't paid. She fell a couple of times and left the house late at night, once because she believed she had a doctor's appointment and once to get wine. I put a latch on the door but removed it for "safety reasons" when asked to do so by a social worker.
>
> Once, she came into the kitchen looking for a paring knife. I asked her if she wanted to pare an apple, and she responded that she wanted it to feed her dog, Topaz. Topaz had been dead for about 20 years. On another occasion,

> she went to eat something from the fridge that was mouldy. Her attention to her personal hygiene declined, and she was occasionally incontinent.

On January 10, 2017, Eleena signed a new power of attorney document before Hilde Deprez at Deprez's office, appointing Tim and Verna as her powers of attorney and representatives in place of Joyce Myler, who lived in Spokane, Washington.

In her file notes about the appointment, Deprez wrote: "Ms. Murray [is] just as feisty and as determined as when I met her before." She noted that "Ms. Murray is a very determined lady with a strong will and optimistic outlook who doesn't want to depend on anyone. She said she'd realized that having Ms. Myler as her power of attorney, someone she trusted with her life, did not make practical sense as she needed someone who was 'here.'" Deprez ended her comments saying, "Ms. Murray was in great spirits but obviously (maybe for the first time) realized that she may not live to be 100 years as she said."

Tim said that, during the meeting, Eleena told Deprez that she wanted to change her will and was told she needed another appointment. Brian recalled the same conversation and said that Eleena had brought her will in an envelope in her purse to the meeting. Deprez didn't recall Eleena saying that she wanted to change her will at the meeting, and her notes for the meeting didn't mention it. She acknowledged that her habit was to have separate appointments for wills.

Tim testified that "on or about January 20, 2017," which was ten days after going to see Hilde Deprez, "I observed that in conversation, Ms. Murray was non-responsive for a minute or so. Her eyes didn't focus on me. I was concerned and drove her to VGH. Ms. Murray had another non-responsive episode in emergency when she was being seen by a neurology resident. Ms. Murray was admitted. I was told that she'd had a seizure."

On her discharge on January 25, Brian and Tim moved her bed to the main floor dining room of her home so that, Tim said, "she wouldn't have to use the stairs."

Brian said in an affidavit that shortly after Eleena returned from VGH, "She said words to the effect of 'I have got to go in and make changes to my will.'"

Hilde Deprez was away from her office from February 6 to 16, 2017. During that time Tim left a message at her office, according to notes by a member of her staff:

> Call from Tim Henderson [phone number].
>
> Informing that Eleena Murray wants to change the Will
>
> Value of the property has changed significantly and more money should now go to family instead of charity.
>
> Appointment for FEB 22 at 10:30 at Eleena's house ▶ 2327 Collingwood Street, Vancouver.

On the date and time set, Deprez went to see Eleena. She said that Brian and Tim were outside, standing on the sidewalk by the gate to the house. She testified: "Ms. Murray said, 'I know why you are here and I have no business for you.'" She was in "no mood to change anything or discuss anything and apologized to me for 'wasting' my time."

In her notes on the encounter, Deprez wrote, "Ms. Murray's resolute approach was as I remembered from my meeting with Ms. Murray when doing the 2013 Will and the Power of Attorney." Deprez also recorded that, as she left, she told Brian and Tim, who were still outside on the sidewalk, that "Ms. Murray didn't have anything to say. They commented that Ms. Murray was 'stubborn' and that the 2013 Will made 'no sense given the value of the house. I told them that it was totally up to Ms. Murray and if she doesn't want to make changes then she doesn't want to.'"

Tim and Brian's version of events differed from Deprez's. Tim denied leaving a message at Deprez's office, saying the value of the property had changed significantly and more money should be going to the family instead of to a charity. Brian said that he and Tim weren't on the sidewalk outside Eleena's home when Deprez came. He said Tim was at work and that he'd gone shopping for a loaf of bread. Tim, however, did not provide his work records.

Under the terms of the 2013 will, any increase in the value of Eleena's home benefitted the BCSPCA, as the recipient of the residue remaining after the specific gifts to Ms. Murray's family, which did not change regardless of an increase in the home's value.

Tim testified that Eleena's physical and mental health deteriorated in February 2017 and subsequently: "She had difficulty managing her hygiene because of bladder and bowel incontinence. She didn't have daily showers or baths but told me she had. She became more confused and agitated as the day went on. Because she refused to accept care workers at her home when I was absent on March 12, 2017 I and Verna tricked her into going to VGH on the basis that doctors needed to look at her heart. There was nothing wrong with her heart, but we didn't think she would go voluntarily."

Eleena was assessed by a geriatric psychiatrist who said that Eleena was suffering from vascular dementia and "needed support." She was soon after transferred to a local long-term care facility.

In early May 2017, her friends Joyce Myler, co-executrix of the 2013 will, whom Tim had kept posted about Eleena's health, and Kim Crawford, came from Spokane, Washington, for a week's visit to Eleena. Before their trip, because of difficulties Crawford had recently experienced with respect to her mother's estate, she suggested that Myler, as co-executor of Eleena's will, review it with Eleena to ensure that her wishes were clearly understood. Joyce and Kim treated Eleena to lunch at the West Vancouver location of the chain Beka Bakery & Café on Thursday, May 4. Myler took a list of the principal bequests in the 2013 will because the original was in Eleena's lock box at her home.

Myler and Crawford said Eleena brought a handwritten, undated, unsigned note on yellow notepad paper expressing her views. The note left out nephews Dan Henderson and Ron Tekano, who'd been in the 2013 will. Eleena said Dan, who lived in the recreational and retirement community of Lac La Hache, a five-and-a-half-hour drive north of Vancouver, hadn't been in touch for years and that she'd had an argument with Ron accusing him of stealing some of her jewellery, which he denied.

On the other hand, the note increased the amount from $60,000 to $100,000 each for her niece Verna, Verna's daughters, Carla and Gina, and

Tim. While the 2013 will hadn't specified a precise amount for the British Columbia Society for the Prevention of Cruelty to Animals, the note said $100,000. Eleena had crossed out a lower figure of $60,000. According to Joyce, Eleena said, "The same as my closest family members, but no more." After paying out all the bequests, there still would be substantial funds in Eleena's estate. It was decided that Eleena's wishes about the allocation of this money would wait until the fall.

Joyce was contradictory about Eleena's mental capacity at the meeting. She said she'd "observed that her brain was slipping a bit and she was forgetful" but also that "she was always a very decisive person, to the point of being prickly or even rude at times. She was decisive and lucid during our meeting at the café, and I didn't have any concern about her understanding of what we were doing." Kim Crawford said that Eleena "was totally with it, very lucid, and showed no signs of cognitive impairment."

From Tim, Joyce learned where the lock box was in Eleena's Collingwood Street home and that Eleena always left a key in it. Joyce put the note in the lock box.

Eleena died five months later, on October 4, 2017. In the period between the lunch meeting and her death, Eleena never went to Deprez or asked her to come to her to change the 2013 will. Nor did she contact any other notary public or a lawyer for this purpose.

When Joyce collected the will and the note from the lock box after Eleena's death, she noticed some changes to the note. Whereas she'd crossed out lines in black ink at the meeting per Eleena's wishes, there were now lines crossed out in blue ink.

In her role as executrix, Joyce put Eleena's house up for sale in May 2020. It sold for $1.9 million; when Eleena made her 2013 will, it had been valued at $1 million — nearly a 100 percent increase in just seven years. No wonder there was intense rivalry over what Eleena's real wishes were.

There was a slew of plaintiffs and respondents in the ensuing court case, *Henderson v. Myler*. The plaintiffs were Brian Henderson; Kenneth Smith in his capacity as executor of the estate of Daniel Henderson, who'd died in September 2018; Gina Hancock Bernier and Carla Hancock Leversage in their capacity as executrices of the estate of their mother, Verna, who died in April 2018; and Ron Tekano. Opposite them were the respondents: Joyce Myler and Elizabeth Jones in their capacity as executrices of Eleena's estate and Gina Hancock Bernier and her sister, Carla Hancock Leversage, on behalf of themselves. Whichever way the case went, they would gain. The other respondents were Timothy Henderson, Eleena's late husband's brother, Don Murray, and nieces Constance Kennedy and Julia Hawks, plus the British Columbia Society for the Prevention of Cruelty to Animals and John Basich, a friend of Eleena's who'd done her many kindnesses, including driving her around. The note left $40,000 to him. He said that when he'd told her, "You don't have to leave me anything," she'd replied, "It's done."

Four issues were debated at the hearing:

1. Was Murray aware of, and did she approve of, the residual bequest to the BCSPCA under the 2013 will?
2. Did the note represent the "fixed and final intention" of Murray to change or alter her 2013 will such that the note was "fully effective" as a valid codicil or alteration to it?
3. Did Murray have the requisite testamentary capacity in May 2017 to confirm the note as a codicil altering the dispositions in the 2013 will?
4. Did Murray know, understand, and approve of the amendments to the 2013 will made by the note?

Brian and Tim testified that Eleena said she wished to leave $5,000 each to Carla's sons, Austin and Jarrod, and mentioned giving funds to the Vancouver Opera, the Playhouse Theatre at the city's Granville Island, and the Queen Elizabeth Theatre. Kim Crawford said she was surprised that Murray left no money for arts organizations.

According to Tim, "In 50 to 100 conversations I had with Ms. Murray over seven to ten years, she told me that she would leave me whatever was left in her estate and/or the Collingwood Home." Neither was left to him in the 2013 will or in the note. Joyce Myler testified that Murray made a comment to her that "Tim wants the Collingwood Home once I pass, but it's not going to happen." Tim also said that Eleena was "consistent" in saying that Brian would receive "something financial" in her will. Brian didn't receive anything in either the 2013 will or the note.

Justice MacNaughton stated:

> The factors in this case that do not support a finding that the Note represents Ms. Murray's final intentions are:
>
> 1. Ms. Murray did not sign the Note, and it was not witnessed. The Note lacks all of the hallmarks of formal validity;
> 2. the Note is not titled, and it does not contain formal language revoking the 2013 Will or expressing an intent to change it and no language to show that the Note was intended to have testamentary effect;
> 3. the Note is not written on formal paper, but on a page from a note pad, suggesting an impermanence or informality rather than a fixed and final intention;
> 4. there is no express revocation of Ms. Murray's 2013 Will or expression of her intention to change or alter it;
> 5. Ms. Murray did not tell anyone about the Note and did not provide a copy of it to her executrices;
> 6. the Note is a mix of Ms. Murray's handwriting and Ms. Myler's handwriting and notations. In some cases, the evidence is unclear as to who made what markings on the Note;
> 7. the Note did not reflect what Ms. Murray said in discussions with family members about the disposition of her estate;
> 8. some of the names written on the Note, and not crossed out, did not have a monetary gift assigned to them, suggesting they were not discussed at the May 4, 2017, meeting and that the Note was a work in progress;

9. the Note is a list of certain names with amounts, and in some cases with no amounts. Another note, containing similar information, was found in the kitchen by Ms. Crawford and thrown out. The existence of several notes, with similar writing, suggests an ongoing thought process rather than a final testamentary intent;
10. when Ms. Murray sought to change her 2010 Will, she wrote directly on the original of the Will. There was no writing on the 2013 Will; a signed copy of it remained in the lock box;
11. the Note does not dispose of the entirety of Ms. Murray's estate or specify what should happen to the residue of the estate.

MacNaughton added:

> Although the plaintiffs make much of the fact that the size of the gift to the BCSPCA in the 2013 Will was unusual and inconsistent with the average testamentary gift to the charity, it is not determinative in the analysis. Ms. Murray had no immediate family. It is entirely possible that she chose to benefit a charity that reflected her love of animals as opposed to extended family members. The question is what Ms. Murray subjectively intended, not what an average person would choose to do with their estate.

She concluded:

> For the reasons given, I answer the questions to be addressed as follows:
>
> 1. Ms. Murray was aware of and approved of the residual bequest to the BC SPCA under the 2013 Will.

2. The Note does not reflect Ms. Murray's fixed and final intention to change the 2013 Will and is not fully effective as a codicil or alteration to the 2013 Will.
3. Ms. Murray had the requisite testamentary capacity in May 2017 to execute the Note as a codicil to the 2013 Will.
4. Finally, Ms. Murray did not know, understand, and approve of the amendments to the 2013 Will made by the Note.

The BCSPCA had won. It was $1.4 million richer. Its lawyer said that he "had been provided with irrevocable instructions from my client to honour the gift to John Basich of $40,000 as set out in the Note in the event that the 2013 Will was found to be Ms. Murray's last will and testament." It was a nice gesture. Basich was the only potential beneficiary excluded from the 2013 will when it and the note were compared.

What happened to the lock box is unknown.

19

LOUIS THE PARROT

Louis was a brandy-swilling, profane, egotistical, bossy, pampered, gorgeous blue-and-yellow pet macaw parrot who inherited a Victoria, British Columbia, mansion and its grounds. They were willed to him by his owner, Victoria Jane Wilson, who died in 1949 at age seventy-one. She never married, was childless, had no siblings or close friends, and was reclusive. Louis was the love of her life, given by her parents on her fifth birthday, her chief companion throughout the years.

The property was in a prime location in Victoria and developers wanted it. Their wish was to tear down the mansion and build lots of high-rise apartments. The will checkmated them because it stipulated that Louis must live out his days in the mansion and that under no circumstances should his environment be disturbed. This meant that the house had to remain standing until the bird dropped dead — and parrots are blessed with very long lives. The standoff lasted seventeen years. Louis became and still is a folk hero to heritage preservationists around the world.

It's an irresistible story that gained international attention — as much for the absurdity of the situation as for the poignant backstory of how Wilson came to bequeath a mansion to her feathered friend.

"Louis roosts in and is the de facto landlord of one of the most sought-after parcels of downtown real estate in scenic British Columbia," *Life* magazine reported in "The Old Bird Won't Sell," a story that appeared in its August 1963 issue. "In the eyes of certain businessmen Louis is a bone in the throat of civic progress."

An only child, Victoria Jane was a lonely little rich girl whose father, J. (James) Keith Wilson, a real estate tycoon, kept her a virtual prisoner in the family home. He did the same with his wife, Kitty, her mother.

Victoria Jane was born one year after Keith and Kitty married in 1877. Kitty, full name Mary Kennethina, was the middle daughter of prosperous Victoria businessman Alexander Munro, who made his wealth as head of the Hudson's Bay Company's BC operations. Like Munro, Keith Wilson was a Scot by birth. He was born in 1846 in Aberdeen, Scotland. In his early twenties he was hired by the Bank of British North America, a big bank with branches across Canada and some in the United States, which merged with the Bank of Montreal in 1918. Keith was entrusted with the assignment to open a branch in Portland, Oregon. After he'd accomplished this, the bank transferred him to its Victoria office. It had been among the first banks to set up operations in British Columbia.

Keith subsequently left banking to enter real estate and became the owner of extensive holdings throughout Victoria, including a number of hotels: Portland, The Ritz, Metropolis, and one he named The Wilson.

In the early years of their marriage, Keith and Kitty were part of the social whirl, and the society column in the *Victoria Daily Colonist* described Kitty as beautifully dressed.

In 1894 Keith was elected an alderman. The next year he ran for mayor. On election day, January 17, 1895, he was punched in the face at the polling station. His attacker was Theodore Lubbe, part owner and manager of a water supply company that Keith had criticized during the campaign. Keith didn't hit back. Both men were then about fifty years old.

Keith came in second in the mayoralty race, but public attention was riveted instead by accounts of the bash to his face. Nothing like this incident had happened in recent memory, if ever, in Victoria, which had carefully cultivated a genteel reputation. Keith filed an assault charge against Lubbe.

The judge, M.W. Tyrwhitt-Drake, declared Lubbe guilty but didn't sentence him to jail. Drake said, "It wasn't a serious assault, though clearly an assault was committed. A sufficient punishment would be a fine of $25 [$750 today] and I give judgment accordingly."

The punch is the origin of why Louis the parrot inherited the mansion. Keith had never been much of a joiner. "He did not associate with a great number of organizations," the *Colonist* said when he died years later, in 1934. "However, he was a keen historian and had a fund of information about everything BC. He was a member of the British Columbia Historical Association where he found an outlet for his enthusiasm for historical subjects. He also was an associate member of the Victoria Real Estate Board and a member of the Pacific Club."

Keith became increasingly insular after the Theodore Lubbe incident and the court's decision not to send Lubbe to jail as punishment. He became more and more controlling with his wife and daughter, isolating them from relatives and friends.

The hilltop mansion and its grounds were so big that there were two entrances a block apart — 730 Burdett at the lower end and 727 Courtney at the top — but Kitty and Victoria were not seen outside of either. Keith encircled the grounds with a tall white picket fence to prevent trespassing.

He suspected all men of being fortune hunters in nefarious pursuit of Victoria's wealth. "When I was a boy I delivered newspapers to her house," James Nesbitt wrote in the *Colonist* on April 27, 1980. "Each afternoon she was at the Courtney Street entrance to her house and took the paper from me over the fence, rarely saying one word, for 50 feet away, stood her father, making sure the paper boy did not run away with his daughter. I often heard Louis cawing like mad, but I never saw him."

According to a 2012 *Victoria Times Colonist* "Tales from the Vault" article by Stephen Ruttan, "On the few occasions when Victoria Jane did leave the house, her father would follow her. He would be hovering in the background, occasionally dodging behind poles if she happened to talk to someone. No wonder she grew up to be painfully shy."

Victoria lived her entire life in the three-storey gabled-roof mansion her father had built, close to the downtown area and the city's inner harbour.

It was nicknamed "The White House" by locals because its exterior was painted white. Within this gilded cage — filled with antique furniture, large crystal chandeliers, heavy gilt mirrors, Dresden china, ornate pillars, and hand-carved staircases — young Victoria Jane Wilson spent her days yearning for companionship.

Visitors were rare, mostly Keith's business associates, and Kitty became estranged from her family. Victoria Jane wasn't allowed to spend any time with her cousins, and she rarely socialized with other children. Mother and daughter often didn't leave the house for long periods of time, giving rise to local speculation that Keith wouldn't allow them out. Thus isolated, the young girl cherished Louis's companionship.

At the time of her death, Victoria Jane possessed sixty parrots of many types, including budgies, lovebirds, and Mexican and Panamanian parrots, but Louis was always foremost as he'd been with her almost her entire life, save for her first five years. Blue-and-yellow macaws such as Louis are among the largest of the parrot species; they weigh between two and four pounds and have five-feet wingspans. They are often intelligent, talkative, good mimics, playful, and entertaining, which is why macaws have been kept as pets for centuries.

An online article titled "Macaw vs Parrot: What's The Difference?" by August Croft on A-Z-Animals.com says, "While all parrot species make fantastic pets, there are a few differences to keeping a macaw vs a parrot as a pet. Many parrot species exhibit more aggression than the average macaw. Macaws enjoy forming close and personal bonds with humans just as much as with other macaws, while some parrots prefer and require bonds with their own kind. However, both parrots and macaws make fantastic pets in a wide variety of homes. They are both extremely empathetic creatures."

Victoria Jane's parrot collection occupied the mansion's entire top floor. It must have been quite noisy with all the birds chattering away. Victoria also owned a cat, Fagan, which presumably she kept at a distance.

Victoria treasured Louis and spoiled him with special treatment. Typically, parrots munch on sunflower seeds, nuts, and fruits and drink only water. But Louis received unconventional extras such as hard-boiled eggs, white grapes — and brandy! Indeed, Louis's alleged guzzling became something of a local legend, with some newspapers bluntly labelling him a "lush." Other reports, though, said he was being maligned and that his annual brandy consumption was only a modest two bottles, doled out daily in spoonfuls.

Victoria bought Louis a companion macaw, carefully selected so that Louis wouldn't feel that his perch at the top of her affections was in peril. *Life* magazine said the bird's name was "Morrie," but a neighbour told the *Victoria Daily Colonist* on August 8, 1963, a few days after the *Life* story was published, "I think they must have made a mistake. I've heard Wong [Louis's caregiver] say, 'Maudie, be quiet,' and then Louis would repeat the same words right after him. Maudie is only 60 years old." Maudie/Morrie was smaller, less colourful, and said little, subservient to King Louis. Louis was always numero uno.

Victoria asked her father to buy her a car, solely so that she could take Louis for short drives. Although he didn't allow his wife and daughter to associate with people, Keith didn't stint on buying things for them, and he bought Victoria Jane a luxury Hupp-Yeats electric automobile.

Louis was ruffled by the sound of the engine, with the result being that the car was put into storage after just a few outings. Following Victoria Jane's death, the car was purchased in 1959 by Stan Reynolds, an Alberta vehicle collector. The car is today displayed in the Reynolds-Alberta Museum in Wetaskiwin, Alberta, which traces the mechanization of transportation, agriculture, and industry from the 1890s to the present. Museum staff have said the car was found in a garage behind a sealed wall in Victoria's mansion and that "great care was taken to delicately remove it without bothering Miss Wilson's pet parrot, Louis, who had his aviary set up in front of the garage." When the car was extracted, it was discovered that it had less than a hundred miles on the odometer.

Louis reportedly had an extensive vocabulary of swear words that would make most humans blush. But where did he pick it up? It's a mystery as Victoria Jane was both refined and genteel. "I've heard some of the things that bloomin' bird says now and again," an elderly Victoria tradesman was quoted in *Life* magazine's 1963 article on the avian celebrity, "and what I can say is you can bet your ruddy home he never learned it from Miss Wilson. She was a proper and kindly lady."

In 1917, when Victoria was forty, her mother died. Subsequently, for many years, Victoria's life revolved around her domineering, aging father, with the two of them living in their mansion secluded from society. Her only break was twice-a-day visits to her birds upstairs.

After her father's death in 1934, Victoria began to venture out in public. She hosted small dinner parties at the city's high-society Empress Hotel and went on occasional shopping binges, wearing a long sable coat in cold weather. Otherwise, her life was very quiet; she never invited people to her home. "She continued to fill her closets with tasteful and expensive clothes, but she rarely wore them," Laura Langston wrote in "Fame Came after Parrot Lady Died," a 1988 *Victoria Times Colonist* article. "Infrequently, she attended an afternoon tea. She was a quiet, soft-spoken woman, always properly dressed and usually seen standing off to the side or in a corner."

In mid-1949 Victoria Jane's health declined. She hired a nurse, and a doctor made regular house calls. On July 8, 1949, realizing that her end was near, Victoria wrote her will. She died at home on July 16, 1949. Her lawyer, John Howard Harman, applied to British Columbia's Supreme Court on September 19 to grant probate of the will, which it did four days later on September 23.

Harman's submission said her estate was worth $408,308.68 (more than $10.7 million today), consisting of the home, blue-chip stocks, Dominion of Canada bonds, two bank accounts, and some real estate holdings. These included property in the heart of Victoria's business district, at the northwest corner of Yates and Douglas streets, on which three stores were located from which she received monthly rent plus the land on which her home was located.

Harman had asked the real estate and insurance firm of Cabeldu & May of Victoria to appraise her possessions. It said about the house:

> The house is well built, of old-fashioned design, possibly built 50 to 60 years ago, but very well kept up and preserved. It has numerous bathrooms and washrooms, three kitchens, entrance hall off Burdett, main hall leading to three good sized rooms. Upstairs there are three main

> rooms with numerous smaller rooms and corridors, heated by hot water oil [water boiler using oil as the heat source] from a detached house connected by companion-way. The house, because of its design and age, and the difficulty of conversion possibly has a detracting effect on the land.
>
> Present Market Value,
> (without chandelier light fixtures) $5,500.00
> House and Land $14,000.00

The inventory of her other possessions started with items she'd accumulated for her birds: for the big — large round, square, oblong, and tall cages and stands; regular and flight cages for smaller budgies, canaries, and lovebirds.

Louis was appraised at $150, the highest amount of all the birds. That's equivalent to $2,000 today, the current top price for blue-and-yellow macaws.

Victoria had drawerfuls of gloves and closets full of clothes and hats, but her biggest fashion extravagances were furs: squirrel, lamb, muskrat, fox, seal, wolf, beaver, civet, but no mink.

Victoria Jane started her will with $2,000 gifts to two women, one of whom, for unspecified reasons, renounced her bequest. The other woman owned a bird supplies store.

Louis wasn't specifically named in the will; the general term "birds" is used, but Louis was famous and the press made him the star.

After the bequests to the two women, Victoria turned to her chief concern:

> I direct my Trustees to hold the rest and residue of my estate for the following purposes, namely:
>
> To make proper provision for the care of my birds and other pets of which I may die possessed
>
> After having made full provision for the care of my said birds and pets to apply the balance of my estate to be put in separate trusts in the name of J. Keith Wilson for:
>
> The British Columbia Protestant Orphanage, $11,000
>
> The Queen Alexandra Solarium for Crippled Children, Cobble Hill, B.C., $11,000

> The Canadian Red Cross Society and the Provincial Royal Jubilee Hospital, "each shall receive one-half of all the balance of my estate not otherwise disposed of."

She then listed "supplementary provisions" for the care of the birds:

> My trustees shall pay a suitable person capable and willing to care for my birds and pets
>
> To allow such person to use my residence as a home for himself and such companions as my Trustees shall approve during the time he or she is caring for my said birds and pets and to pay all necessary heating expenses and other normal expense in connection with the upkeep of my said residence and to supply to him or her sufficient bird feed supplies and veterinary attention so that my pets may be properly cared for.

"Miss Wilson loved those birds," a neighbour told the *Victoria Daily Colonist*. "She wanted them to be warm in winter. That's why she arranged things as she did."

Wilson wound up: "Notwithstanding anything herein contained I expressly authorize and empower my Trustees to sell or rent any part or parts of my house and of the garden and grounds on which my house stands if in the opinion of my Trustees such part or parts are not needed or necessary for the proper maintenance and care of my said birds and pets."

One of the two witnesses was Yue Wah Wong, the estate's gardener. John Harman as Victoria's executor asked Wong to be the birds' caretaker. Wong agreed, which meant he still had a job. He was paid $250 a month, a goodly sum, equivalent to $3,270 today. Wong gave Louis the same deluxe treatment as Victoria had — brandy and his special diet of walnuts and hard-boiled eggs.

"Hard-Drinking Parrot Stymies Progress," the *Calgary Herald* wrote in 1959. "100-Year-Old Parrot Still Soaks Up Brandy in Victoria," the *Vancouver Sun* wrote in 1961.

The city of Victoria was aflutter with pride when popular U.S. magazine *Life* spotlighted Louis. The magazine's 1963 homage to Louis was written by Russell Sackett, a follow-up to a 1957 article he'd written. He wrote, "I first met Louis in 1957; I wanted to see the noted squatter. I was reassured by a view of Louis, brilliant blue and yellow, looking splendidly indestructible even through a dusty, heavily screened window of his private house, where he was doing a headstand on his perch."

Sackett decided to pay a return visit in 1963 to see how Louis was faring. Checking in at the Empress Hotel, he met a long-time Victoria resident in the lobby who wondered whether Louis actually was dead and had been replaced by a doppelgänger.

Sackett telephoned Wong, who invited the journalist to come to the estate, look through the window, and see for himself. Sackett wrote in his article: "Feeling unsure and jittery as I squeaked through the gate, I walked to the window, shaded my eyes and tentatively called 'Louis?' There was a shadowy movement far back in the birdhouse, and suddenly there was Louis, jaunty and resplendent as ever, sidestepping deliberately along his perch toward the window. 'Wong?' he rasped, eyeing me accusingly."

Victorians told Sackett that Louis pined for Victoria and could be heard calling, "Miss Wilson, Miss Wilson, I want some water." Some said that Louis would demand, "Wong! Damn you Wong! Where are you?" He did have a reputation for profanity.

Soon after Victoria's passing, Douglas Abrams, an apartment developer, making use of the clause in Victoria's will that "a part or parts" of her estate could be sold, bought the house and its surrounding land, saying his intention was to build a high-rise apartment complex. But he'd overlooked the clause in the will that stipulated that Louis must live out the rest of his days in the home — and that under no circumstances must his environment be disturbed. This meant that The White House, including its then-attached aviary, heated from the same furnace system as the house, had to remain standing until Louis dropped dead.

Louis was then eighty-six. Calculating the actuarial odds, Abrams figured Louis's days were numbered.

Meanwhile, he turned The White House into six apartment units and waited for the old bird to die. He should have done some research on the average lifespan of macaws; based on it being a hundred years or more, Louis was far from his final days. Russell Sackett wrote in his *Life* article: "Louis callously recovered from the pain of his mistress's passing, and to Abrams's rueful astonishment, seemed to take a new lease on life."

The apartments' occupants were elderly ladies who enjoyed getting together for afternoon tea every day in the building. They told acquaintances that it could be hard to hear one another because of Louis's screeching. Their practice was to squint for a glance of Louis through a peephole in what they said was a padlocked steel door of his premises.

Abrams waited nine years for Louis to croak before giving up. Louis had outwitted him. Abrams sold the property to two Victoria businessmen who said they were willing to wait out Louis. Louis outsmarted them, too; he was one of those macaws with a longer-than-average lifespan. The developers, it seemed, were the real birdbrains.

Louis was rumoured to want to be left alone by the public. He apparently disliked having his picture taken — flashbulbs put him in a foul mood, and when he was in a foul mood, he swore a lot. The last published picture of him was in *Life*'s 1957 article. It showed Louis on his brass parrot stand, his wings fully extended, an overhead grip bar, and a smiling Wong standing beside him, one hand on the side of the stand and a shut window behind him.

As the years flew by, Louis outlived all of Victoria Jane's other birds. His continued existence was of annoyance to the three charities Victoria had designated in her will because she'd stipulated that any residue left would go to them after "full provision" for her birds. Moreover, her will disqualified anyone who contested it:

> I further direct that if any person or beneficiary of this my will shall oppose or attempt to oppose my Trustees in the exercise of their powers or duties or in purported exercise thereof of in actual or purported exercise of any power discretion or attempt by any means to obtain

> payment of my benefit hereunder prior to the date upon which my Trustees deem payment proper and appropriate then any such gift or any balance thereof to any such person or beneficiary shall pass to a charitable purpose or object or charitable purposes or objects nominated in writing by my Trustees, such nomination to be made by my Trustees at the date when full or partial payment in their discretion be proper and such charitable purpose or object or charitable purposes or objects so nominated shall be subject to the provisions of this my will in like manner as if named herein.

All this legal jargon boiled down to "Hands Off."

Each year a representative of the Royal Jubilee Hospital, one of the three charities named in Victoria's will as an eventual beneficiary, paid a visit to see if Louis was still ticking. From time to time, a member of Harman's law firm, the administrator of the estate, dropped by for the same purpose. A.C. Wurtele, chairman of the board of the Royal Jubilee Hospital, expressed his displeasure about the restriction when he was interviewed in 1966: "It seems to me that people are more important than parrots and Louis might well be handed over to the Society for the Prevention of Cruelty to Animals. This money is being wasted. The estate is being eroded by legal fees, and I am afraid there will be nothing left."

Wurtele had made a good point. The same year, 1966, Victoria's law firm decided to evict Louis, saying it was too costly to keep him in the large house, which had fallen into decay. It made arrangements with Yue Wah Wong for the aging Louis to be cared for by Wong and his family at their home, a modest abode in comparison to Victoria's White House.

In 1969 *Canadian Magazine* published "The Bird Who Has It Made," which described how Louis continued to live a privileged, pampered life. Wong had died soon after taking Louis in, but his family continued to care for Louis in the grand manner to which he was accustomed.

With Louis kicked out, developers were free to demolish the house and erect high-rises. The house was demolished at the beginning of June 1972.

In an article published June 9, 1972, in the *Victoria Daily Colonist*, reporter Erith Smith wrote:

> Victoria Wilson's house on the hill on Burdett Street, overlooking the Empress Hotel and Crystal Garden, is no more — and it vanished in almost complete silence despite the howls of horror raised when its end was predicted.
>
> Actual demolition last week required only 20 minutes, but the dust from its 80-year-old crannies hung like a cloud for hours.
>
> Victor Wilson, no relation but present owner of the property has only one regret. "Just the night before demolition someone got in there and stole every single thing of any real value: mirrors, some stair railings and their decorative knobs, some leaded windows, even the big front door and its interesting lock. One person parked outside, nipped in and pulled a soap dish from a bathroom wall, nipped out again, and drove off!
>
> "We thought we might save the trees remaining on the property and the wall along Burdett. It was impossible. The trees proved rotten, and the wall in a state of decay."
>
> Wilson's views on the preservation value of the old house are shared by Victoria archivist Ainslie Helmcken. Both agree historic buildings should be preserved, but not buildings that have merely stood in the city a long time.
>
> Chief claim to fame of the building, the two say, is the fact for that for years it was the home of a parrot, Louis, who with his daily tot of brandy won international renown. Otherwise the Wilson house was just a house simply built about 1890, with wings, rooms, and gingerbread added at the whim of Miss Wilson's father.
>
> Cries for its preservation were due mainly to two factors: Louis, and the house's location in a prominent spot downtown where it could be seen by every passerby.

> On the site Victor Wilson plans to build a 161-unit apartment complex 140 feet high. It will have three levels of underground parking, a sauna, indoor swimming pool, and a hobby room.

The exact date of Louis's death is unknown; some say that he died a few years after Wong, but others say he held on until 1985, when he would have been about 115 years old. By then Victoria Jane had been dead thirty-six years.

While Louis is gone, his legend lives on. In 1975, the Chateau Victoria Hotel & Suites was built near the former White House site, complete with a top-floor restaurant named the Parrot House after you-know-who.

And today, Victoria's Hallmark Heritage Society's highest prize for heritage preservation is called, you guessed it, the Louis Award.

ACKNOWLEDGEMENTS

The chapter on Louis the parrot is an expansion of a story I suggested and wrote that was published by *Canada's History* magazine with the title "Something to Squawk About" in the August–September 2020 issue (pp. 42–46). The editorial director then was Mark Reid; thank you again, Mark.

Many thanks also to Jonny Allen, Royal BC Museum & Archives, Victoria, British Columbia; Robert Anderson, Reference Librarian, Literature Department, Los Angeles Public Library — Central Library; Al Stanton-Hagan, Art Gallery of Ontario Archivist, Edward P. Taylor Library & Archives, Toronto; and Gina Dewaele, Elgin County Archives, St. Thomas, Ontario.

As well as Archives of Ontario; Toronto Reference Library; Boris Laskin Law Library; University of Toronto; University of Saskatchewan Law Library; and librarians at a host of libraries across Canada.

And Bob Harris, Vancouver, an acquaintance through Crime Writers of Canada to which we both belong, who took the ferry from Vancouver to Victoria to make copies of the Dunsmuir and Victoria Jane Wilson wills at the Royal BC Museum & Archives.

Plus, the hard-working, talented team at Dundurn Press and the admirable editor Carrie Gleason.

BIBLIOGRAPHY

Cases

Bautista v. Gutkowski Estate, 2023 BCSC 1485 (CanLII).
Bolianatz Estate v. Simon, 2005 SKQB 40 (CanLII).
Bolianatz Estate v. Simon, 2006 SKCA 16 (CanLII).
Bunn Estate, Re, 1992 CanLII 8220 (SK CA).
Canada Trust Co. v. Ontario Human Rights Commission (CA), 1990 CanLII 6849 (ON CA).
Canadian Association for Free Expression v. Streed et al., 2015 NBCA 50 (CanLII).
Dalla Lana Estate, Re, 2020 ABQB 135 (CanLII).
Fox v. Fox Estate, 1996 CanLII 779 (ON CA).
Gregoire v. Cordani, 2020 BCSC 276.
Grewal v. Litt, 2019 BCSC 1154.
Gust v. Langan, 2020 SKQB 42 (CanLII).
Henderson v. Myler, 2021 BCSC 1649 (CanLII).
Jerry Ellis, Substituted Administrator of the Estate of Nick Bolianatz v. Irving Simon, 2006 CanLII 35599 (SCC).
Jung v. Poole Estate, 2021 BCSC 623 (CanLII).
Kan v. Cheong, 2024 BCSC 1633 (CanLII).
Langseth Estate v. Gardiner, 1990 CanLII 7935 (MB CA).
McBride, Re, 1980 CanLII 1962 (ON SC).
McCorkill Estate v. McCorkill, 2015 CanLII 14497 (NB CA).

McCorkill v. Streed, Executor of the Estate of Harry Robert McCorkill (a.k.a. McCorkell), Deceased, 2014 NBQB 148 (CanLII).
McGrath v. Joy, 2020 ONSC 7454 (CanLII).
McGrath v. Joy, 2021 ONSC 316 (CanLII).
McGrath v. Joy, 2022 ONCA 119 (CanLII).
Millar Estate, Re, 1937 CanLII 10 (SCC), [1938] SCR 1.
Murley Estate, Re, 1995 CanLII 10513 (NLSC).
Nova Scotia (Attorney General) v. Lawen Estate 2021 NSCA 39 (CanLII).
Peach Estate, Re, 2009 NSSC 383 (CanLII).
Ramsden Estate, Re, 1996 CanLII 3709 (PE SCTD).
Rempel Estate, Re, 1922 CanLII 483 (MB CA).
Royal Trust Corporation of Canada v. The University of Western Ontario et al., 2016 ONSC 1143 (CanLII).
Spence v. BMO Trust Company, 2015 ONSC 615 (CanLII).
Spence v. BMO Trust Company, 2016 ONSC 196 (CanLII).
Streed v. McCorkill, 2014 CanLII 6638 (NB CA).
Tataryn v. Tataryn Estate, 1994 CanLII 51 (SCC), [1994] 2 SCR 807.
Tufford, Re, 1984 CanLII 2016 (ON SC).
Vout v. Hay, 1993 CanLII 5 27 (ON CA).
Vout v. Hay, 1995 CanLII 105 (SCC), [1995] 2 SCR 876.
Wishart Estate, Re, 1992 CanLII 2679 (NB KB).

Archives

ARCHIVES OF ONTARIO

Charles Vance Millar. MS 584, Reel, Estate File 55697.
Goldwin Smith. MS 584, Reel 756, Estate File 21824.
Harriet Smith. MS 584, Reel 1822, Estate File 22382.
Robert Dunlop; William Dunlop. MS 921, Reel, RG 22, Series 298, Estates Files, Goderich (Huron), 1842–55.

ART GALLERY OF ONTARIO ARCHIVES

Art Museum of Toronto, Letters, 1900–11. Files J, L, S, W.
Art Museum of Toronto, Minute Book, 1900–13.
The Grange, Documents, Box 55, Files 5, 7, 13.
The Grange, Newspaper Clippings, Box 66, Files 4, 7, 10.

ROYAL BC MUSEUM & ARCHIVES

Alexander Dunsmuir. Will, Reel # B08947, Frame 1861.

Robert Dunsmuir. Will, Reel # B08947, Frame 1829.

Victoria Jane Wilson. Will, Reel # B17349/13671/1949.

UNIVERSITY OF TORONTO ROBARTS LIBRARY

Robarts Library Microtext Collection (CIHM 61759) — Province of Lower-Canada, district of Montreal, Court of Appeals, 1825, November term Francis Desrivieres, James McGill Desrivieres, the Honble. William McGillivray, executor, &c. & &c. and again the said Francis Desrivieres, intervening party, appellants and the Honble John Richardson & al.

Robarts Library Microtext Collection (CIHM 94165) — Extract from the will of the late Hon. James McGill with the charter of the University of McGill College, and the address, delivered by the Principal, on the occasion of the opening of that institution, September 6, 1843.

Secondary Sources

"'Ada' Viola Ada Gardiner: Obituary." Clarke's Funeral Home, March 2, 2017. clarkesfuneralhome.com/obituary/Ada-Gardiner.

Assigning the Ceremonial Name "Harriet Boulton Smith Way" to Part of John Street. City of Toronto Report for Action, February 28, 2017. toronto.ca/legdocs/mmis/2017/te/bgrd/backgroundfile-101934.pdf.

Baird, Craig, host. *Canadian History Ehx* (podcast). "The Great Stork Derby." August 1, 2023. canadaehx.com/2023/08/01/the-great-stork-derby/ca.

Ballard, Clell G. "Lugged Wheels: On the Road to Trouble." *Farm Collector*, September 10, 2019. farmcollector.com/farm-life/lugged-wheels-zmcz19octzhur/.

Bowen, Lynne. *Robert Dunsmuir: Laird of the Mines.* XYZ Publishing, 1999.

Bruni, Cassandra. "A Strong Endorsement of Testamentary Freedom: Spence v BMO Trust." *CanLII Connects*, March 17, 2016. canliiconnects.org/en/commentaries/41241.

"Bursaries for Catholics Not Discriminatory." *Human Rights Digest* 1, no. 3 (April 2000): 7–8. canlii.ca/t/t19h.

Byrne, Mrs. Wm. Pitt (Julia C.). *Curiosities of the Search-Room: A Collection of Serious and Whimsical Wills.* Chapman and Hall, 1880.

Chiasson, Marc-Antoine. "McCorkill v. Streed, Executor of the Estate of Harry Robert McCorkill (a.k.a. McCorkell), Deceased, 2014 NBQB 148 (CanLII)." *CanLII Connects*, October 6, 2014. canliiconnects.org/en/cases/2014nbqb148.

CJN Staff. "Judge Voids Neo-Nazi Sympathizer's Will." *Canadian Jewish News*, June 6, 2014. thecjn.ca/news/judge-voids-neo-nazi-sympathizers-will/.

"Conditional Wills." Guest and Gray Law Firm. guestandgray.com/practice-area/conditional-wills-attorney-texas.

Corporation of the Town of Lincoln. By-Law No. 2017-36. lincoln.ca/media/6133.

Davis, Ivor. "Acrimony and Intrigue Spawned by Pickfair's Lavish Pickings." *Globe and Mail*, January 24, 1981, D7.

Dermody, Colleen. "Ruling From the Grave — Are Conditional Gifts in Wills Valid?" Devry Smith Frank LLP, September 2, 2022. devrylaw.ca/ruling-from-the-grave-are-conditional-gifts-in-wills-valid/.

Ellwand, Geoff. "An Analysis of Canada's Most Famous Holograph Will: How a Saskatchewan Farmer Scratched His Way into Legal History." *Saskatchewan Law Review* 77, no. 1 (2014): 1–26. canlii.ca/t/t0wk.

Frost, Stanley B. *James McGill of Montreal*. McGill-Queen's University Press, 1995.

Goldenberg, Susan. "Something to Squawk About." *Canada's History*, August–September, 2020, 42–46. canadashistory.ca/explore/politics-law/something-to-squawk-about.

Graham, W.H. *The Tiger of Canada West*. Clark, Irwin, 1962.

Krahn, Cornelius. "Rempel, Cornelius (1856–1921)." *Global Anabaptist Mennonite Encyclopedia Online*. Last updated August 20, 2013. gameo.org/index.php?title=Rempel,_Cornelius_(1856-1921)&oldid=77197.

Krahn, Cornelius, and H. Leonard Sawatzky. "Old Colony Mennonites." *Global Anabaptist Mennonite Encyclopedia Online*. Last updated February 24, 2021. gameo.org/index.php?title=Old_Colony_Mennonites&oldid=170107.

Orkin, Mark M. *The Great Stork Derby*. General Publishing, 1981.

"Oscars of Pickford, Husband Belong to Academy, Jury Rules." *CBC Arts*, December 16, 2008. cbc.ca/news/entertainment/oscars-of-pickford-husband-belong-to-academy-jury-rules-1.751810.

Rattray, William. *The Scot in British North America*. Vol. 2. Maclear, 1881.

Reksten, Terry. *The Dunsmuir Saga*. Douglas & McIntyre, 1991.

Southern Poverty Law Center. "National Alliance." splcenter.org/resources/extremist-files/national-alliance.

Southern Poverty Law Center. "William Pierce." splcenter.org/resources/extremist-files/william-pierce/.

Stamberg, Susan. "How Movie Darling Mary Pickford Became the Most Powerful Woman in Hollywood." *NPR*, February 27, 2018. npr.org/2018/02/27/589061990/mary-pickford-darling-of-the-silver-screen-to-major-hollywood-force.

Van Harn, Carol. "Malahide – Burdick Cemetery." Elgin County Branch, Ontario Genealogical Society, March 20, 2014. elgin.ogs.on.ca/ancestor-indexes/cemetery-transcriptions/malahide-burdick/.

Vyhnak, Carola. "Once upon a City: The Frugal Life and Lavish Last Wishes of Thomas Foster." *Toronto Star*, December 13, 2015, IN6.

Whitfield, Eileen. *Pickford: The Woman Who Made Hollywood*. University of Kentucky Press, 1997.

Wilton, Elizabeth Marjorie. "*Bearing the Burden: The Great Toronto Stork Derby 1926–1938*." MA thesis, Dalhousie University, 1994.

INDEX

ABOUT THE AUTHOR

Photo by Edward Macdonell

Will Power is Susan Goldenberg's eleventh book. Her most recent previous book, *Deadly Triangle*, about the 1935 murder of architect Francis Mawson Rattenbury and trial of his wife and chauffeur, was also published by Dundurn Press, in 2022. She has won a Canadian Authors Award and a Canadian Business Editors' Award. She lives in Toronto. Visit goldensusan.com for more information.